TV AND SCHOOLING

Edited by
David Lusted & Phillip Drummond

British Film Institute Education Dept.
in association with
University of London Institute of Education

First published in 1985 by
British Film Institute
127 Charing Cross Road
London WC2H 0EA

British Library Cataloguing in Publication Data

TV and schooling.
  1. Television broadcasting — Study and Teaching
  I. Lusted, David   II. Drummond, Phillip
  302.2'345   HE8700.6

  ISBN 0–85170–180–9

Cover design Mike Leedham

Typeset by Type Generation, London
Printed in England by Garden House Press, London NW10

CONTENTS

NOTES ON CONTRIBUTORS

John Cain is an ex-BBC Controller, Public Affairs, currently research historian with Asa Briggs in the BBC History of Broadcasting Unit. He writes here in a personal capacity.

John Caughie is Lecturer in Film and Television Studies at the University of Glasgow.

George Donaldson is Deputy Head of Archbishop Michael Ramsey School in London.

Phillip Drummond is Course Tutor, MA Film and TV Studies for Education, University of London Institute of Education.

Richard Dyer is Lecturer in Film at the University of Warwick.

Bob Ferguson is Head of Media Studies, University of London Institute of Education.

Anne Hennessey is Head of Miles Coverdale Primary School in London.

James Learmonth is a member of HMI, which convened the committee that produced the DES Report, *Popular TV & Schoolchildren.*

David Lusted is an Adviser in the Education Department at the British Film Institute.

Len Masterman is Lecturer in Education at the University of Nottingham and author of *Teaching About Television.*

Margaret Matheson is a film and TV producer; she produced a quartet of films scripted by David Leland including 'Made in Britain'.

Philip Simpson is Head of BFI Education.

Tana Wollen is a Teacher of English and Media Studies – at North Westminster Community School at the time of writing, currently at George Orwell School, London.

ACKNOWLEDGMENTS

We wish to acknowledge a number of contributions in connection with this publication and its origins.

We start by paying recognition to the group of teachers who produced the DES Report *Popular TV & Schoolchildren* published in April 1983. This Report, which gave rise to massive media coverage, reintroduced television and schooling as terms in a renewed debate over culture and education for the early 1980s. The attention it received led us to reprint the Report as Appendix to this publication. For permission to do so, we thank the DES. (The Report is *Crown Copyright*, and is reproduced here with the permission of the Controller of Her Majesty's Stationery Office.)

Secondly, we record our gratitude to the broadcasters, critics, academics and teachers who gave generously of their time to respond to the Report by contributing to the Television and Schooling Conference jointly organised by the British Film Institute and the University of London Institute of Education in November 1983. The contributors were Sarah Boston, John Cain, John Caughie, Richard Dyer, Bob Ferguson, Anne Hennessey, James Learmonth, Margaret Matheson, Philip Simpson and Anthony Smith. Many of those contributions appear in the following pages in a substantive or modified form, together with others solicited separately. We additionally acknowledge the contributions to debate of the 300 delegates who attended the Conference.

Thirdly, we would like to thank those who worked on Conference organisation. For their able stewardship at Conference, our thanks go to the following members of the Institute of Education MA course in Film and Television Studies for Education: Jane Arthurs, Brian Childs, Michael Conway, Mary Eyton, Bob Fox, Sally George, Mary Hamill, Chris Hibbs, Liz Hill, Bill Lewis, Di Makris, Tony Mitchell, Sui Ng, Derek Reid, Sandra Sinfield, Paula Weiman-Kelman. We also wish to thank Susan Gibbons (Institute of Education) and Julie Maher (British Film Institute) for their considerable organisational contributions.

Finally, we wish to record our debt to those who worked on the preparation of this publication. In particular, we thank Julie Maher (BFI) for her supportive energy and skills in the preparation of essays for publication, together with other members of the BFI: Geoffrey Nowell-Smith, Patience Coster, Roma Gibson, John Smoker and Diana Watt. Special thanks to Tise Vahimagi for acquisition of stills and Jim Adams for selection and provision of frame-images. Thanks also to Tina Foulkes.

Reproduction of stills and frame-images by kind permission of Thames Television (*Minder, Widows, The Benny Hill Show, The Kenny Everett Video Show*); BBC (*Top of the Pops*) and Kieran Prenderville (*Tomorrow's World*), Terry Wogan (*Blankety Blank*), Janet Ellis and Michael Sundin (*Blue Peter*), Sue Lawley (*9 O'Clock News*) and Kate Nelligan (*Licking Hitler*).

David Lusted
Education Department, British Film Institute
Phillip Drummond
Department of English and Media Studies,
University of London Institute of Education
Co-Organisers, *Television and Schooling Conference*, 1983

EDITORS' PREFACE

This book is not yet another scandal-monger on the effects, real or imagined, of television on children or even schooling. It is about setting new terms for developing education *about* television. An impetus to this issue has already been given, following the overwhelming public exposure given to a Department of Education and Science Report, *Popular TV & Schoolchildren*. The pages that follow are intended to promote and extend not only consciousness but also understanding. We have assumed our readership to be a general one but equally recognise specific concerns of those working in the broadcasting and, particularly, educational institutions.

One purpose of this volume is to publish the proceedings of the 1983 'Television and Schooling' Conference. It serves to remind participants of the nature of the day's debates, and to inform those unable to attend. But the act of publication is not one of mere recording. In turning 'Television and Schooling' into a book, we wanted to re-emphasise central questions raised by Conference, but still awaiting fuller answers. How should the institutions of television, and of education, speak to one another? In what senses can television be understood as 'educational'? What are the ideologies of television – and of education? Most importantly, what constitutes education about television?

The essays here address these issues from a number of perspectives. Following this preface and Philip Simpson's introduction, we begin with a context offered by the DES Report *Popular TV & Schoolchildren* which eventually led to this publication. We hear professional broadcasters' responses to the issues raised and offer a range of critical essays on the debates at large. We conclude by entertaining proposals by teachers and educators. What emerges is less 'academic' analysis than a working volume, from a variety of institutional interests, offering sometimes tentative proposals, sometimes fully-fashioned argument. The challenges are clear, but perhaps the most productive forms of response are less so.

Part I reviews events in and around the DES Report and begins with 'A History of Suspicion: Educational Attitudes to Television'. David Lusted probes the cultural prejudices which have inhibited the fuller development of Television Studies in our schools. He detects a two-fold resistance – an endemic 'suspicion of popular forms' coupled with a liberal commitment to 'moral guardianship'. In their place he advocates the critical study of television in the sense of the 'acquisition and use of practices of production and skills of analysis' grounded in an autonomous programme of teacher training and in-service courses.

Having set the scene, this section continues with James Learmonth, the HMI most closely involved in organisation for the DES Report, describing the production of the Report and explaining the authors' sense of being misrepresented in the popular press on the counts of evaluation, effects, and censorship. He further suggests that one unexpected feature of the coverage was its misunderstanding of the views about television of the Report's authors. A contributor to the Report, George Donaldson, teases out two central recommendations – that teachers, parents, and broadcasters should find better forums for discussion about television (perhaps through consultative committee structures), and that Media Studies should be a concern for the whole curriculum.

The Report itself can be found in Part V of this volume. Further substantial critical accounts of the Report can be found in 'Talking about Television' by Bob Ferguson, Phillip Drummond and Manuel Alvarado in *Changing English: Essays for Harold Rosen* (Margaret Meek and Jane Miller, eds., Heinemann/University of London Institute of Education, 1984) and also in 'Feeding the Panic and Breaking the Cycle' by David Lusted in *Screen* (Vol. 24, No. 6, November/December 1983). David Lusted's critical account also reviews the considerable press coverage following publication of the Report.

Part II, 'Broadcasters' Perspectives', permits us to hear influential voices from the world of television itself. Margaret Matheson urges sterner concentration from both broadcasters and educators. She demands for television 'a radical critique from its consumers'. This should be based, she argues, on an educational initiative in 'Television Studies' aspiring to nothing less than the 'imaginative awe' which, in a different context, Auden saw as the basis of the experience of poetry.

John Cain makes a similarly even-handed, if at points provocative, case. Firstly, television must provide 'high-quality' audio-visual material for schools; secondly, it must offer a 'responsible critical base' for its material; thirdly, it must 'engage actively with educators and others in the debate about television and radio and their role in society'. Media Studies, in turn, must beware of polemic masquerading as academic research and of 'tendentious and ideologically simplistic arguments which are bad scholarship and a disservice to real education'. Here, in Cain's animus against the work of the Glasgow University Media Group and the Open University *Mass Communication and Society* course-book, we see opening up some of the more substantial intellectual and political differences between the various contributors to the Conference and to this volume.

Part III, 'Critical Perspectives', offers general critical accounts of television viewing.

Richard Dyer's contribution, 'Taking Popular Television Seriously', attempts to expand the conventional range of meanings for the terms 'entertainment' and 'representation' as they figure in the DES Report. 'Entertainment', he suggests, can take at least two forms: 'escapism' and 'confirmation'. In respect of the former, we need to understand 'the dynamics of pleasurable escape into television' experienced in relation to such diverse programmes as *Top of the Pops* and *Tomorrow's World*; as far as 'confirmation' is concerned, we need to understand the divergent tendencies – of the 'consensual' and of the 'deviant' – from which television weaves its ambiguous endorsements. Four cases of 'representation' are discussed. Does television simply represent, or does it mediate? How does 'representation' connect to notions of typicality and stereotyping? Whom does television 'speak for' and what do audiences 'make of' TV representations?

In 'Children's Television: The Germination of Ideology' Bob Ferguson takes a hard line on the questions raised by Richard Dyer and, especially, on the achievements of broadcasters. The fostering of 'critical consciousness', he asserts, has never been on the broadcasters' agenda, for children's television inhabits an 'established universe of discourse' which is predominantly 'Anglo-centric, often racist, sexist, royalist, pro-capitalist, ostensibly Christian' and encourages belief in charity rather than social change. Children's television thus lays the ground-work for 'the ideological development so necessary to produce audiences for the vacuous and the reactionary'. What must be sought, he argues, is a plurality of viewpoints, alternative ways of conceptualising the world and of articulating media messages. As well as *Blue Peter*, he canvasses an oppositional 'Red Peter'.

A complementary angle is provided by John Caughie in his contribution, 'On the Offensive: Television and Values'. Here the debate over social values and the media is reopened within Media Studies, but this time from a left perspective, in contrast to the right-wing positions which have often dominated this field. Caughie argues that there is no such thing as a 'definitive way of watching television regularly', and he rejects the twin notions of an 'abstract television' viewed by an 'homogeneous audience'. Television, he maintains, should not merely be regarded as 'a source of contemporaneity' on the one hand or of 'control and inoculation' on the other. Rather, in establishing the television process as a system not only of 'flow' but of *hierarchisation*, educational-ists should teach more broadly about 'representations, about ways of reading images, about audiences, and about the ways in which television relates to other institutions of culture and of the State'.

Part IV, 'Television, The Media and Education', offers a range of general and specific accounts of education's role, concluding with concrete suggestions for progress. Tana Wollen resists educational antipathy towards the media and any exaltation of the 'purification processes' represented by schools. In 'Television, Media Studies, and Schooling' she explores 'high' and 'low' cultural estimations of the learning process and traces the left-liberal evolution of educational attitudes to media which are now confronted by the apparent impasse of BEC/TEC provision, MSC/YTS ideologies, and the narrow definitions of the mooted 'core curriculum'. She places emphasis upon the opening up of Television Studies through notions of representation, which should be studied in its characteristic 'movement from image to history', and entertains the validity not just of Television Studies or Media Studies, but of the broader project of Media Education at large.

Practical proposals of differing kinds are offered by Anne Hennessey and Len Masterman. Hennessey, in 'Starting in the Nursery: Why Teach about Television?', points to a crucial absence in the DES Report: nursery education was the only sphere of schooling not addressed. Infants, she reminds us, are in the business of learning not only basic skills of numeracy and literacy, but are engaged in the very process of learning to 'read' television itself. Institutionally, she notes, the 'across the curriculum' ethos of the nursery school, serviced by multi-specialist teachers, and not hampered by the timetable/curriculum fragmentation of the secondary school, seems likely to provide a more open and a still more challenging arena for the introduction of a new kind of Television Studies.

Len Masterman makes similarly concrete proposals in his discussion of 'Future Developments in TV and Media Studies: An Ecological Approach to Media Education'. Like Hennessey's, his interests are strategic rather than epistemological, but his concern is less with an ignored sector of the schooling system than with the outgoing links between the schooling system, the family, and the media institutions. It is thus an holistic or 'ecological' approach and, in contrast to Hennessey's concern for the younger learner, Masterman is concerned with media education as a 'lifelong' activity. The axes of his plan are: relationships between media educators and parents; relationships between media educators and media personnel; the question of 'training' for media practitioners and media educators; and, as a supraeducational 'community' focus, the notion of the 'media centre' as a key modern social institution.

Collectively, these contributions establish terms and offer strategies to develop new and co-ordinated directions in relations between the television and education institutions. The pressing need now is for formal arrangements to continue debate and plan courses of action. All interested parties must ensure that education about television faces contention and, avoiding a fatally haphazard development, proceeds by design.

INTRODUCTION

PHILIP SIMPSON

The essays collected here enable readers to confront some fundamental questions about television and schooling, and they propose some directions to be followed in the search for answers. Differences of emphasis and even outright disagreement can easily be drawn from the essays: contributions were deliberately solicited from a *range* of educationists and television practitioners, and nobody sought or expected a false consensus.

In this introduction I want to note some of these contradictions and to suggest that both the DES Report *Popular TV & Schoolchildren* and the consequent conference at which many of these papers were first presented set out clearly the matters and modes for future action.

Matters
Essays presented here look afresh at questions of effects and values in relation to television and its audience. The Conference was not another occasion for the much exposed question-of-effects routine: we are not even within sight of measuring television's effects on people, young or old, through any widely-accepted research methodology appropriated from the social sciences. This is not said to dismiss empirical analyses; it is more to remind ourselves, as George Donaldson does,[1] that such analyses have their limitations, as most of their advocates readily acknowledge.[2] As with the longer established tradition of educational research, only the more quantifiable effects are at all easily measured, and what these measurements mean is not always self-evident. With television, too, longer-term consequences are difficult to assess; with both educational and television research, teachers have to act on the assumption that the ways in which the relationship between the student and the world is represented, either in television or through education, fundamentally influences her or his attitude to the world. Among the analogies drawn between education and television in these essays,[3] the recognition that both television and schooling deal with *representations* of the relationship between the student and the world is fundamental. Understanding such a relationship cannot ever be based solely upon quantifiable factors, however much these offer.

1

From this observation it is a short step to the more contentious matter of values and judgements, and the ways in which these are involved in understanding how television represents the world. John Caughie[4] forcefully argues through some of the most awkward issues that any teaching about television has to confront. Seeking to distance themselves from the kinds of sectarian or moral and political outrage over television which have so much damaged relationships between teachers and television practitioners, and eschewing that suspicion of popular forms which characterises much English teaching,[5] media teachers have sometimes emphasised theory and methodology and left out the importance of television studies in disclosing the values by which society lives. What is awkward about Caughie's argument is that it refuses to see values as 'the abstractions of truth and beauty' which are based upon an assumed consensus of moral or aesthetic truth and which can be read off television's many 'texts' or found in their contents or intentions. He insists instead that their values are to be found as much in the way television addresses its audiences and the conventions by which television organises its output; he challenges the convenient fiction that there exists 'an' audience for television whose members have the same set of social values as each other and the broadcasters. For Caughie, television is 'bad' not simply when it fails to reach some professional standard of production or critical crestline of aesthetic value assumed to be generally shared, but when it is oppressive and exploitative of specifically-defined fractions of the television audience. More positively, he proposes that some forms of representation and some images can, by such social criteria, be found worthy of support and circulation:

> What we are doing when we teach in this way is to investigate in precise, specific and interrogative ways the forms in which television reproduces, inflects and recirculates in its representations the relations of power which are there already in society.[6]

The awkwardness for teachers in this analysis of values in television is the obligation to confront, with care and skill, questions about power in society, for there are few models of good practice in this matter in the subjects for which teachers are trained.

Questions about values and television cannot be faced, then, unless we attend to what John Caughie calls 'the forms and practices and routines of television as a whole'. But a tendency towards abstraction in teaching about television has to be guarded against: as Margaret Matheson says, even zoology would be dreary if it were only about how zoos are managed. Both Caughie and Richard Dyer propose that such teaching is also about the experience of 'reading' the representations offered by television, in the programmes it labels as 'entertainment' as much as those which are offered as 'serious'.

Both critics raise questions about representation and entertainment in relation to all kinds of programmes, but there are differences in their approaches which repay attention. Caughie asks us to see, through careful attention to the modes as well as the matters presented, the ways in which values are immanent in television, and to recognise the social values by which these are to be judged. Dyer, however, is hesitant to make evaluative judgements until the matter of experience has been explored a little more. In his view, we need a better understanding of why and how programmes are pleasurable, and the ways in which one programme may offer different pleasures to different groups or individuals. For him, the dialogue between teacher and student begins with open-ended questions about the kinds of pleasurable entertainment offered as much by *Tomorrow's World's* jaunty technology as by *Top of the Pops'* self-conscious sexuality. Explorations about the appeal of these programmes must precede any attempt to uncover the meanings which are assumed to lie behind appearances and to be, covertly or overtly, reworking or reiterating social values.

In contrast to the difficulties which the issues raised by Caughie present, not least to teachers, Dyer's emphasis upon teaching through the exploration of experience is appealing, partly because the basic teaching approach is so familiar: you show the programmes and then you discuss them. But, as Dyer indicates, if the experience is to be treated seriously, discussion begins from an agenda set by the teacher, and his own brief account of the access to experience offered by the concept of representation is a useful model. Moreover, we could add, since television is more than the sum of its visible parts, questions about the scheduling of programmes, the routine practices and conventions of television, its relationships to other institutions and agents, cannot easily be broached through viewing experience alone. Yet these have identifiable effects upon what is offered to the viewer.

John Caughie and Richard Dyer usefully confront some fundamental questions about what might be taught about television and why, but they both make clear that much remains to be said about *how*.

Modes

How *is* television to be taught in schools and colleges? The papers published here don't answer this question in a way that would enable an interested teacher to start teaching about television next week. One reason for this is that there is no one answer: most teachers would first have to argue with senior staff for the timetable space and resources to teach about television, and no single syllabus proposal could meet such diverse needs or opportunities. Another reason is that Len Masterman's book *Teaching about Television*[7] and other publications, some by the BFI,[8] offer specific approaches to aspects of teaching television, including the important area of practical work with video.[9] Teaching about

3

television is not widespread however; there is no established orthodoxy and no extensive apparatus of public examination. As a result, there are insufficient teaching materials which draw upon sustained classroom experience.

Other reasons are more complicated and draw us into some of the points made here by James Learmonth, Anne Hennessey, Tana Wollen, and Len Masterman. *Popular TV & Schoolchildren*[10] appears at a time when those concerned with the study of television do not know their place. Only twenty years ago Paddy Whannel and Stuart Hall set out in *The Popular Arts*[11] to convince teachers that topics like film and popular music deserved a place in the school curriculum. Film Studies was eventually, if limitedly, accepted as an autonomous examinable subject of study, not merely as an option for the unruly or a way into discussing bicycle theft or war and peace. Over the same period of time, television supplanted film as the popular entertainment medium, but it soon became clear that the arguments for including film in the school curriculum couldn't simply be repeated for television. Film Studies concentrates almost exclusively upon narrative fiction films; Television Studies has to embrace situation comedy, news, sport, soap opera and other forms. Film in the school context can be treated like the other arts in many respects; television has obvious affinities with media like radio, newspapers, magazines and advertising.

Even more than film, television's variety makes it susceptible to misuse or misplacement in the timetable as a useful visual aid, a transparent 'window on the world'. All this means that the struggle to define and secure teaching about television has usually been subordinated to the concern to claim curriculum space for Media Studies as a subject which could usefully place together film, television, video and other media that teachers felt able or constrained to offer.

As Len Masterman writes,[12] establishing Media Studies has been successful in some senses: in secondary and tertiary education it has become a coherent discipline with its characteristic concepts, practices and modes of enquiry. It has also become, though, a typical special option. Although many polytechnics offer degree courses with substantial and popular Media Studies options at degree level, most schools timetable the subject in that twilight zone of subjects which don't have enough life to be part of the common core but are not so dead as to be rejected by the students themselves. Media Studies does sometimes secure a timetable slot because it can take its place as a part of the English curriculum, or as one of the subjects which the Hargreaves Report[13] designates as for 'personal and social education'. Manpower Services Commission initiatives have eroded much of the time available for this kind of education, but some courses under the Technical and Vocational Education Initiative legitimately incorporate work on the media.

4

But the essays mentioned above are not arguing about the best curricular space for Media Studies; what they explore is a more thorough-going mode of media education. *Popular TV & Schoolchildren* proposes the fundamental change which they elaborate: 'special courses [of Media Studies] are not enough: all teachers should be involved in examining and discussing television programmes with young people'.[14] Anne Hennessey sees the nursery/infant classroom as already providing a possible context for such discussion: 'Talk is encouraged in nursery/infant classrooms, and teachers . . . have time to talk to children. Children talk a great deal about the television programmes they watch at home, and nursery and infant teachers are usually skilful listeners'.[15] (Her view contrasts sharply with the recent HMI document *English from 5 to 16*[16] where television discussion is a desirable objective only for 16-year-olds!). Len Masterman sketches out what the point of discussing television programmes in subjects like Geography might be, and Bob Ferguson forcefully insists that a critical consciousness needs to be brought to bear by pupils on the kinds of children's television programmes which already provide a reference point for much classroom work.

The argument being made is that Media Studies might remain in the space it already has but a more extensive programme of Media Education needs to be undertaken across the curriculum and the age ranges. The emphases vary: the DES Report wants television programmes discussed more widely in schools, whereas Len Masterman suggests that television, video and other packages of educational 'software' are being used in more schools and these, too, need critical attention. But both proposals would entail a radical revision of the kind of work undertaken in teacher training as well as a reappraisal of the materials produced.

We need to be a bit cautious here. Across-the-curriculum initiatives do not seem to have been successful even when the arguments are as powerful as those in support of language development. Furthermore, Media Studies is not just the name of a potential subject discipline: it implies a strategy for curriculum innovation through which teachers can be trained and supported in arguing for time, resources and status.

Given the right circumstances and central government support, Scottish media teachers have demonstrated that Media Studies is a bridgehead into the curriculum which is worth securing for its own sake,[17] and other gains have followed. Media education might prove to be the general line of advance that media teachers have wanted, or it could prove to be the bridge too far. The next step must be a fuller examination of what 'media education' or even 'television education across the curriculum' actually means in terms of specific pedagogic aims, objectives and practices, and in terms of education and political strategies.

One strategic initiative was provided by *Popular TV & School-*

children, endorsed by the Conference and confirmed in Len Masterman's signposting of future developments.[18] This calls for more collaboration between television practitioners and teachers, and the participation of broadcasters John Cain and Margaret Matheson underlines the value of such collaboration. Their contributions show, though, how uneasy relations between teachers and practitioners tend to be once the 'cordon sanitaire' of educational television is left behind. Collaboration has to negotiate tensions and differences like those revealed in the essays by John Cain and Bob Ferguson once the general output of television is the subject.

Such negotiations are never done once and for all, and some arrangement needs to be made whereby *media* teachers and practitioners can meet regularly to discuss each other's work without the gladiatorial atmosphere which interventions by the National Viewers and Listeners Association seem to encourage. The BBC and IBA already have consultative bodies, but other formal arrangements are required where detailed exchanges between broadcasters and teachers specially interested in the general output of television can meet.

The Conference provided an instance where genuine exchanges might have developed: John Cain, from a very different perspective, seems to join in a view shared by John Caughie and Richard Dyer that the 'general sense' younger viewers are assumed to derive from television needs to be examined much more closely. Cain also notes the impasse now reached through the conflict of ideologies about bias. A long-term project for regular and less combative exchanges between teachers and TV practitioners will not end this kind of impasse, but it might clarify for both sides and third parties the nature of the disagreements and distinguish between what, say, the NVALA, the Glasgow Media Group and cultural critics like Caughie and Dyer are saying.

Len Masterman's survey of the ecology of television makes a number of proposals which the DES and the BFI at least ought to act upon. He is right to suggest, too, that teaching about television is too important to be left to those with merely a professional interest in the matter, and his vision of Media Centres developing lifelong media education for the whole community should be taken seriously.

The spirit in which Masterman writes also informs the essay by Umberto Eco from which two of the writers in this document quote. That essay ends with a beginning:

Let us meet with others and watch television critically together, confronting our reactions and speaking face to face about what television has taught us or has pretended to teach us. Don't switch off television, switch on your critical freedom![19]

References

1. George Donaldson, 'Teachers and Television: The Right to Comment', pp.24-28 below.
2. Michael Tracey, 'Television affects everything we do, everything we think', *The Listener*, 19 January 1984.
3. See the articles by George Donaldson, Anne Hennessey, Margaret Matheson and Tana Wollen in this collection.
4. John Caughie, 'On the Offensive: Television and Values', pp.53-66 below.
5. The history of this suspicion is outlined by David Lusted in this collection.
6. John Caughie, cit., p.66.
7. Len Masterman, *Teaching about Television*, Macmillan 1980.
8. See *Teaching 'Coronation Street', Starters* and *'Hazell Meets The First Eleven' Slide Pack*, together with *Teaching Situation Comedy* (forthcoming), all from BFI Education.
9. Len Masterman, 'Future Developments in TV & Media Studies: An Ecological Approach to Media Education', pp.87-92 below; also Manuel Alvarado 'Practical Work in TV Studies', BFI Education document.
10. *Popular TV & Schoolchildren*; The Report of a Group of Teachers, DES April 1983, reprinted on pp.95-121 below.
11. Paddy Whannel and Stuart Hall, *The Popular Arts*, Hutchinson 1964.
12. Len Masterman, 'Future Developments' cit., pp.87-92 below.
13. 'Improving Secondary Schools: Report of the Committee on the Curriculum and Organisation of Secondary Schools' (The Hargreaves Report), ILEA, March 1984.
14. DES Report, cit. Reprinted in this collection, pp.95-121.
15. Anne Hennessey, pp.85-86 below.
16. *English from 5 to 16*, Curriculum Matters No. 1, An HMI Series, DES 1984.
17. Described by David Butts, Research Fellow in the Media Education Research Project in Scotland, in his report dated September 1984, available on request from the Department of Education, University of Stirling, FK9 4LA.
18. Len Masterman, pp.87-92 below.
19. Umberto Eco, 'Can Television Teach?', *Screen Education* 31, Summer 1979.

PART I
THE CONTEXT

1. A HISTORY OF SUSPICION: EDUCATIONAL ATTITUDES TO TELEVISION

DAVID LUSTED

Preamble
It is worth recalling the Report of an influential conference organised by the NUT in 1960 called *Popular Culture and Personal Responsibility*.[1] A very 1960s title. If there are any copies still lying around, they're worth dusting down and re-viewing, not least to contrast with the debate and opinion in the pages of the more recent DES Report, *Popular TV & Schoolchildren*.[2]

Both reports are notable for an *assembly* of views. They act as a forum for debate, as distinct from a research project or a learned paper with a coherent argument and a set of concluding recommendations. The recommendations in the DES Report really amount to calls for even further debate and describe conditions under which further debate could productively take place. This common feature of the two Reports, from their own key moments of educational change, may or may not be related to the widespread media coverage both met but it certainly makes them landmarks in the history of educational attitudes to television.

Where the Reports differ is in their focus. For the NUT Report, the issue was the *effects* of television, a very familiar theme. For the DES Report, the focus is on the 'images of adult life' on television. That shift from a set of worries about television's effects to a set of questions about television's representation of the social world is central and absolutely crucial. It must be held to as a direction for the future of schooling about television.

The Research
The outstanding research into what teachers think about television remains that by Murdock and Phelps, published in 1973 and titled *Mass Media and the Secondary School*.[3] The research finds four approaches to television among their sample group of teachers. The most overwhelming approach, of the largest number of teachers, is that television is irrelevant to the classroom and therefore it is not considered or talked about at all. A second approach, by fewer teachers, was that since television was harmful teachers had a duty to do one of two things. Either they actively excluded it, so that they effectively joined that first

11

group by not talking or thinking about it, or they brought aspects of television into the classroom in order – to use a term from film studies – to inoculate children against it. Very few teachers inhabited the fourth approach, which was to teach *about* television in any positive way.

Murdock and Phelps found that the positive attitude was not only in the minority but that English teachers were especially guilty of anxiety about television and, crucially, about television's effects. The effects they were most worried about were mainly on language ability and what's termed in the Report 'imaginative expression'. Interestingly, science teachers tended to think television's effects were – on the whole – good in providing certain kinds of factual information that they saw supporting their own teaching in the classroom.

One other point from the research: it found, not too surprisingly, that the social position and cultural formation of most teachers is at a distance from what the majority of the population actively choose to watch on television and therefore what the kids they teach watch. In other words, there's a culture gap between teachers and taught. Ten years on, my guess would be that this is changing but I think it has not changed that much and that it is changing very slowly.

Probably a majority of teachers are ill at ease with the issue of education about television, and a central problem is how that can be changed. Obviously, there are agencies in and around the education system making raids into teachers' consciousness (and the advances in cultural theory and cultural criticism over the past ten years add fuel to that). But something much more systematic is necessary; less guerrilla raids, more a general strategy across the spectrum of schooling. The focus needs to be on policymakers, with a view to devising a central policy to legitimate the issue of education about television.

The first requirement is to understand the basis of resistance to television amongst teachers a little better. I suggest two components to consider. One concerns a set of popular views about teaching as an aspect of moral guardianship. That connects in a particular way with the issue I'll raise first: the long-standing cultural history of suspicion of popular media and popular forms.

Suspicion of Popular Forms
Television is commonly regarded with suspicion. There is a long history of which that suspicion is only the most recent development. Ed Buscombe, in his IBA Fellowship research in 1974, wrote:

Both poetry and the novel were once denounced as frivolous, time-wasting and even corrupting. And all of these changes were levelled at the English theatre in the hey-day of its achievement. In just such terms the new art forms of the twentieth century – cinema, jazz, radio and now television – have been attacked.[4]

As well as going back a long way, the lurid, inflammatory vocabulary deployed and the assumptions founding it are worth scrutiny. From 1851, when theatre was the main target, the *Edinburgh Review* offers a none-too-rare example:

> One powerful agent for the *depraving* of the *boyish classes* of our towns and cities is to be found in the *cheap* shows and theatres, which are so specially opened and arranged for the attraction and *ensnaring* of the young. When for 3d a boy can *procure* some hours of vivid enjoyment from exciting scenery, music and acting . . . it is not to be wondered at that the boy who is *led on the haunt* then becomes rapidly *corrupted* and *demoralised*, and seeks to be the doer of the infamies which have interested him as a spectator.[5] [my emphases]

Clearly a great deal of emotional energy, as well perhaps as a tint of tabloid sensationalism, is invested in statements like these, through a language of seduction and entrapment. Why popular media, of all the multifarious aspects of social and cultural conditions, should be considered such a central determinant of the way people lead their lives is by no means self-evident. The culture gap is clearly a factor: the fact that the class with the power to speak authoritatively speaks with no authoritative *experience* of popular media and the culture of the class that has. But, more, it is in some complex way bound up with an equivalent deep-rooted cultural suspicion, with just as long a history, of youth – especially male, working-class youth – and children. The earliest appropriate reference I've found shares much of the language of the above and its assumptions about 'the boyish classes':

> The young people of today love luxury, they have bad manners, they scoff at authority and lack respect for their elders. Children nowadays are real tyrants – they no longer stand up when their elders come into the room where they're sitting, they contradict their parents, chat together in the presence of adults, eat gluttonously and tyrannise their teachers.[6]

Cultural suspicions go back a long way. That is Socrates.

The 'suspicion complex' of popular cultural forms and youth is a key component of the continuing serial of moral panics about television. Moral panics are fed by a combination of consensus journalism, behavioural research and religious/moralist lobbies. They take various forms but frequently one of three:

worries about television's representation of violence feeding imitation;

worries about television depressing a disposition towards intellectual enquiry;

vaguer worries about television contributing to declining 'moral standards'.

I've written elsewhere of how the press response to the DES Report misplaced the report into just such a moral panic about television.[7] Two points are worth making, however.

Clearly, television must have effects, but it is doubtful that they can be grasped through moral, spiritual or behavioural frameworks alone. (Certainly, enough money and indignation has been expended over the years in order to try to prove otherwise.) Nor is it likely that these areas are as important as social or ideological factors when it comes to understanding what television's effects are, as certain recent studies indicate.[8]

The second observation, most importantly, is that it is doubtful if any schooling based on a suspicion of television can have much to do with education. It's hard to think of any other subject, or social or material phenomenon around the curriculum, that schools study out of suspicion. Other motivations seem more useful. Accounting for television's popularity is an obvious one; accounting for the pleasures it offers and the meanings it makes. These are more scholarly frameworks, suggesting modes of enquiry that treat television as a key contemporary medium, rather than as an agent of social disease. The close textual and institutional analyses necessary to this discipline are, to its credit, encouraged by the DES Report. It is only the closer identification of the features of the discipline that is required.

Traces of the dominant teacher attitudes and cultural suspicions located here can be found in certain formulations in the DES Report but they are always circumscribed by sets of concerns that arise from its concentration on the brief to explore images of the social world on television. There lies its novelty and strength. It is that brief which forces the authors to actually look at the television programmes in a way that the approaches of behavioural research and the moral lobbies do not allow. It forces close attention to the programmes themselves and not just to isolated moments or worries about the act of looking itself. It considers what the viewers think about television and what they use it for, rather than extrapolating, as many academics do, from an irregular experience of television-viewing and what regular viewers say. That is a novelty in educational (indeed any) approaches to television.

Teaching as Moral Guardianship
The second founding feature of teacher resistance to television lies in a set of popular views about teaching as an aspect of moral guardianship. It is a view of the *role* of the teacher as priest as well as disseminator, a kind of gate-keeping role, allowing into the schoolroom only rigorously scrutinised and authorised bits of the world outside. The picture I have in mind is of a First World War poster in which Britannia, back to wall, protects a Britain composed of little figures against the soldier Hun who – with pointed bayonets, hats and moustaches – breaks through the

14

door. Similarly picture the teacher in the popular imagination, protecting the little ones from pointed barbs of culture – television, comics, cinema, etc. – slipping like the Blob through the gaps in windows and doors (caused by education cuts?) of the contemporary classroom. What I'd like to see is a change in that kind of popular image so that, instead of a gate-keeping role, the teacher introduces the outside world into the classroom in a spirit of enquiry rather than suspicion.

It needs to be recognised that the view of teacher-as-moral-guardian is a legacy from the confusions of purpose in the founding moment of the British state education system – an alliance of conservative interests in social and economic control, liberal interests in protective legislation and the mobilisation of a popular movement for literacy. It is inscribed in a particularly forceful way in the history of humanities teaching in Britain, and especially in the teaching of English. This is Denys Thompson, in *Discrimination and Popular Culture* in 1964:

> There are, of course, many schools that teach their pupils how to understand the language of advertising, to read between the lines of the press, to *discriminate* between films, to *go shopping* on TV and to see the difference between *good and bad design* in town and country. All schools should give some instruction of this kind. As it is, school-leavers are too often *a ready prey* for the mass media. Everything learned at school in the way of aesthetic and *moral training* is contradicted and attacked by the entertainment industry. The aim of schools is to provide children with *standards* against which the *offerings* of the mass media will appear *cut down to size*.[9] [my emphases]

Thompson is part of a great tradition of argument about the importance of literary studies in the classroom. That sense of moral guardianship and suspicion of popular forms – a cut above but none the less reminiscent of the language of the *Edinburgh Review* – comes unavoidably, particularly acutely, through it.

As well as reminding ourselves of particular groups of teachers, like English teachers, whose cultural formation is part of that tradition of suspicion, it is also useful to relate them to a whole string of educational reports.

Educational change – but also state thinking – in Britain can be charted by these educational reports, known best by the names of the chairpersons of the committees that produced them: Crowther, Spens, Newsom, Plowden and Bullock. All draw attention to the ignored need for visual media like television to become facts of curriculum life although only Newsom and Bullock more than stated the need. In 600 pages of Crowther, for instance, there is just one key sentence in only one paragraph on the whole issue of culture and schooling. It is probably no

15

more than an afterthought but its terms set the scene for subsequent
Reports:

> The free *play* of those cultural and *anticultural forces* which *permeate*
> the modern world through newspapers, books, cinemas, wireless and
> television . . . the *bewildering* and *bludgeoning* nature of the *impact*
> made by the mass media of communication . . . the reasons why we
> can't be content that so many intelligent young people should be *left*
> *without a guide* through the maze.[10] [my emphases]

The terms of cultural suspicion ('the bewildering and bludgeoning
nature of the impact') founds the role of the teacher here: less 'a guide
through the maze' than a priest in the minefield.

The thoroughgoing evaluative tone of the quotations, from the
Edinburgh Review through to Crowther, softens when we arrive at
Newsom, with its talk of its focus group, 'the less-able pupil', 'imbibing'
television (Paragraph 465).[11] The key phrase is:

> We should wish to add a strong claim for the study of film and
> television in their own right, as powerful forces in our culture and
> significant sources of language and ideas . . . (Paragraph 474)

The drink metaphor in the choice of the term 'imbibe', with its
temperance fear of insobriety, is avoided in the key phrase, with its
emphasis on *study*.

While Newsom gives over several paragraphs to television, by the
time of Bullock television has become a considerable presence with
many references. Newsom's concern with study returns in Bullock with
altogether more consideration. Still, however, symptoms of the familiar
suspicion abound. Ponder on the inflection here for instance:

> . . . a school should use [television] as a disseminator of experience . . .
> developing a critical approach [which places] the emphasis on
> *extending and deepening* the pupils *appreciation* . . . (Paragraph
> 22.14).[12] [my emphases]

With its emphasis on 'a critical approach', Bullock appears more
investigatory than paternalist, but still a sense of valuation resides in
the formulation, making 'appreciation', rather than 'understanding',
paramount.

The DES Report too – to bring us up to date – is crossed by confused
traces of concern and interest as variants of suspicion and aspects of
unhelpful moralisms and paternalism. There are seeds of quite another
approach, however, and it is these that need nurturing.

16

Television Education as Critical Study
Any kind of evaluative approach to schooling about television is inadequate, whether its purpose is a celebratory 'appreciation' or, more likely, discrimination within it or inoculation against it. Nor are approaches that treat television as a hobby or a vocational or instructional practice valid alternatives. The only proper television education in the secondary and further education sectors is, echoing Newsom, as a form of *study*.

Let me float the notion of a *critical study*. I don't mean by that fault-finding, the 'picking of holes' in television, nor do I mean a form of criticism from some impossibly objective position from where all of television can be surveyed without ever experiencing its production. What I mean is a study of television as the acquisition and use of practices of production and skills of analysis. Importantly, these skills and practices are to be seen as integrated, so that learners know where they come from and how they fit together. The object is to come to know arguments about the status of what are to be seen as different styles of practice and analysis whose consequence constitutes television as an object of study in different ways. Such a course of study should include applying types of textual and social analysis, discerning different aesthetic practices, investigating television history and its institutions. And also, and importantly again, exploring the various social and cultural understandings that we have of television. Studying television is not just an exploration through practice and practical criticism, but through positions which are as much there for study themselves so that their origins and meanings are understood, too. That is obviously a tall order, but it's not as tall as it sounds, and there's a lot of that kind of teaching about television going on in schools all over. If you're living in Scotland now, it's official policy; in the Scottish education system media studies is a curriculum fact.

Conclusion
In this analysis of education's prevailing attitudes to television, that sense of suspicion seems to me to be startling and needs to be worked against. English teaching is one natural (or at least appropriate) home for schooling about television, since the teaching of English and Television share a concern with language and analysis. However, the teacher/taught culture gap referred to earlier and the history of English teaching suggest certain incompatibilities so that relation is not one 'in essence' nor strategically necessary.

There are shifts in teacher style as well as attitude attendant upon the approach I'm promoting. And it may be as well to view the existing organisation of knowledge in the curriculum, as expressed in the present arrangement of subject-teaching, as itself subject to change. There is nothing sacrosanct about today's curriculum, nor about the role of English in tomorrow's. It may be that a new emphasis on *language teaching* would transform thinking about where the sites of language are; from the present almost exclusive print-dominated media, like novels and other forms of print-publishing, to audio-visual media like cinema and television.

At this time, then, the most appropriate emphasis should be on an autonomous programme of teacher training and in-service courses. There is, for instance, the Grunwald Declaration, a UNESCO document published in 1982. It says this:

> We call upon the competent authorities to initiate and support comprehensive media education programmes from pre-school to university level and in adult education, the purpose of which is to develop the knowledge, skills and attitudes which will encourage the growth of critical awareness and consequently of greater competence amongst the users of electronic and print media.[13]

The questions attendant upon this are: Who, in the case of Britain, are 'the competent authorities', and what do I, they, we intend to do about schooling and television?

References

1. *Popular Culture and Personal Responsibility: Verbatim Report of a Conference, National Union of Teachers, October 1960.*
2. *Popular TV & Schoolchildren: The Report of a Group of Teachers*, DES April 1983, reprinted on pp.95-121 below.
3. Graham Murdock and Guy Phelps, *Mass Media and the Secondary School,* Schools Council, Macmillan, 1973.
4. Ed Buscombe, 'TV Studies in Schools and Colleges', *Screen Education* 12, Autumn 1974, p.5.
5. 'Juvenile Delinquency', *Edinburgh Review* 1851, pp.403-4 (quoted in Graham Murdock and Robin McCron, 'The Television and Delinquency Debate', *Screen Education* 30, Spring 1979).
6. Socrates, quoted by Michael Brake in *The Sociology of Youth Culture and Youth Sub-Cultures*, Routledge and Kegan Paul, 1980, p.1.
7. David Lusted, 'Feeding the Panic and Breaking the Cycle', *Screen* Vol. 24, No. 6, Nov-Dec 1983.
8. See, especially, David Morley, *The 'Nationwide' Audience*, BFI TV Monograph 11, 1980, and Dorothy Hobson, *'Crossroads': The Drama of a Soap Opera*, Methuen, 1982.
9. Denys Thompson, *Discrimination and Popular Culture*, 2nd Ed., Penguin, 1974.
10. Report of the Central Advisory Council for Education (The Crowther Report), HMSO, 1959, paragraph 510.
11. *Half Our Future*, Report of the Central Advisory Council for Education (The Newsom Report), HMSO, 1963(4).
12. *A Language for Life*, Report of the Committee of Inquiry (The Bullock Report), HMSO, 1975.
13. *The Grunwald Declaration*, UNESCO, January 1982.

2. ORIGINS AND AFTERMATH OF 'POPULAR TV & SCHOOLCHILDREN'

JAMES LEARMONTH

In January 1982 Sir Keith Joseph, the Secretary of State for Education and Science, asked HMI to convene a group of teachers to report on the values and images of adult life presented in a series of popular evening BBC and ITV programmes. He hoped that the report would encourage and inform serious discussion of the issues raised among professionals in education and television, parents and the general public.

It is important to be clear about the purpose of the study: it was never intended as a definitive research project into the values which television makes available to young people, nor did it claim to represent (in a social scientific sense) teachers' reactions to television. The report was intended as a considered response from fifteen teachers of widely differing backgrounds to what they perceived during a five-week period of viewing. It was intended as a contribution to a debate about the role of the teacher in pupils' experience of television which subsequent meetings, conferences and, indeed, this publication continue to develop.

The group was asked to report within six months. Contrary to some press reports, the teachers who took part in the study did not have five weeks off school simply to watch television. They watched programmes in addition to their normal school duties, and set themselves a rigorous routine. During the viewing period in March/April 1982 there were always at least two of the group watching a selected programme; reports were written immediately after viewing and collated at the end of each week. There were discussions at all levels during the compilation and drafting of what was to become *Popular TV & Schoolchildren: The Report of a Group of Teachers*. The group recognised from the start that the brief given would not allow a definitive statement about values in popular television to be made and tried to reflect in the style of the Report's writing the diffidence of the judgments offered. It was a relief, after the first hysterical reaction to the Report in the press, to read in the *Listener* of Peter Fiddick's recognition of that attempt.[1] In seeking to raise issues rather than bury them, the group often expressed its views in the form of questions, or with careful qualification, or openly acknowledged that members held differing views.

Throughout the study, the teachers received valuable support from the BBC, the IBA and the ITV companies, and consulted with the programme-makers, heads of departments and one controller. Some of these came to the group's meetings and answered questions. Research in the sociology of broadcasting had made it clear that different people may perceive the same television programme in quite different ways and then put that experience to quite different uses, so the teachers asked pupils in their schools to comment on the programmes. Pupils' views of the programmes were included in the Report not only because in at least some cases they differed from the teachers', but also because the group felt strongly that their inclusion would underline their belief that children are not passive and uncritical viewers but very often have clear and sophisticated opinions about what they see.

The composition of the teachers' group, which included representatives of each phase of schooling except nursery, underlined HMI belief that it was important to draw on the concern and experience of a wide range of teachers rather than only on the expertise of those involved in media studies in secondary or further education. This in no way implied disrespect to those teachers who have for many years been developing the theory and practice of media studies. The group saw it as important to consider how teachers might respond to children's experience of television from the age of five onwards, and this broad approach (together with the timescale given) made impossible any exploration of a common theoretical framework from which the group might proceed.

Such was the media reaction to the Report on its publication in June 1983 that it became difficult to disentangle the Report's real findings from those attributed to it. The group felt misrepresented by the popular press on three important topics:

1. *Evaluations* The teachers did not intend the Report as an attack on television. The vocabulary used in press coverage, however ('slam', 'lash', 'accuse', 'target', 'condemn', 'attack', 'slapped wrists', and, inevitably, 'TV stars get a caning'), suggested that the teachers categorised programmes into 'good' and 'bad', and judged the majority to be the latter. In fact the structure of the Report was chosen to consider themes, not individual programmes.

Will anyone who has not read the Report now believe that the group very much enjoyed watching *Minder*, that it commended in the Report *Minder*'s honest approach to showing the consequences of physical violence, and applauded its 'positive moral impetus and richness of script, humour and character' (p.103, below)?

2. *Effects* Banner headlines, with inverted commas to suggest direct quotation, reported 'Children "are being corrupted by shows"' (*Daily Mail*, 22 June 1983). Yet throughout the Report, the group was careful

Minder's honest approach to showing the consequences of physical violence . . .

. . and its positive moral impetus and richness of script, humour and character.

not to make general statements about the effect of television on children because the teachers felt it unlikely that fifteen teachers in five weeks could make a valid contribution to a controversy which has already involved social scientists in lifetimes of research. Nevertheless, in redefining the nature of the Report, the press ensured that latecomers to the debate did not find what they had been led to believe was there: one Sunday newspaper found the report 'predictably unilluminating' in its attempts to 'measure the influence of television on children' (*Sunday Telegraph*, 26 June 1983).

3. *Censorship* Almost inevitably, after the emphasis on values and effects, the press concluded that the group was recommending more forms of censorship in broadcasting. The only time the word is mentioned in the Report is in one of the conclusions where its context makes it clear that the group explicitly distanced itself from the concept and favoured a much more ambitious, complicated and gradual approach. The teachers found the processes of viewing and discussing, both within the group and with broadcasters, a highly educational one, and one of their recommendations is that this sort of discussion should be conducted much more widely amongst teachers, producers, parents and pupils. Where criticism of programmes is offered in the Report, the group's recommendation was for diversification rather than restriction, particularly in the context of the way in which particular social groups like ethnic minorities or women are portrayed.

What, then, were the conclusions of the teachers?

First, they enjoyed and found much to commend in many of the programmes viewed. They tried to avoid falling into the trap of conferring greater value per se on programmes which set out to educate and inform than on those whose primary aim is to entertain.

Second, they took the view that mainstream broadcasters too often separate the responsibilities to educate and entertain into self-contained boxes. Within the broadcasting organisations, there seemed an assumption that schools and continuing education programmes were where education took place, and that it was somehow confusing to suggest that children learnt from general output programmes. The Report does not suggest that entertainment programmes should be didactic, with improving social messages attached to them, nor does it underestimate the proper concern of broadcasters to retain their professional independence and judgment. But the group sought a clearer acknowledgment from mainstream broadcasters that their professional responsibilities included educational responsibilities, and saw no conflict in broadcasters protecting their professional autonomy while at the same time exercising those responsibilities.

Third, the teachers saw a need for broadcasters, teachers and parents

22

to review their different but related responsibilities with reference to popular television, especially necessary in a changing social and technological context in which there may be two or more television sets per house, video, and the imminent arrival of cable. These reviews should take place in formal meetings and should recognise a need for them to be sited in different regions.

Fourth, while acknowledging much good work already done, some of it involving the broadcasting organisations, the group sought a much greater role for teachers in responding to their pupils' experience of popular television. Specialist courses in media studies represent one approach, but all teachers should be involved in examining and discussing television programmes with young people.

The teachers who contributed to *Popular TV & Schoolchildren* expressed their judgments about values in popular television programmes with diffidence. Even so, their insistence on diversification of programmes rather than restriction, on debate rather than legislation, is unequivocal. They sought 'a richer, more varied coverage of human experience' (p.112, below) and looked forward to urgent debate about the relative responsibilities of parents, teachers and broadcasters. The success of the Report will be measured by the extent and nature of that debate.

Reference

1. Peter Fiddick, 'Do parents and children see TV in the same way?', *The Listener*, 30 June 1983, pp.10 and 22.

3. TEACHERS AND TELEVISION: THE RIGHT TO COMMENT?

GEORGE DONALDSON

Teaching is an act of faith. Teachers measure success in terms of formulas learned, essays written and examinations passed. Yet wider aims cannot be measured: the development of individuals in self-knowledge and in their relationships with the world.

The parallels between teaching, thus defined, and television are obvious. We have become obsessed with measuring the effects of television. In the twenty years since the medium was established the number of studies devoted to assessing its influence, whether on the level of violence in society or on personal sexual mores, is enough to stock a library. We also persist in believing that television is an effective educative medium. The BBC's commitment to 'inform, *educate*, and entertain' remains the formula most frequently quoted to describe the purpose of television. Yet none have succeeded in proving whether – or how – television has effects on people, let alone in measuring those effects.

I was one of the authors of *Popular TV & Schoolchildren*, all of whom came to the subject convinced that television does have effects on youngsters and that how it does so is a matter for public concern. Nothing we saw in the course of our studies and deliberations changed that belief. There was no more unanimity in the committee about the influence of television than could be found amongst the authors of previous studies or any random selection of the viewing public. But we did agree that television presents powerful images of reality and that those images are significant for children.

When the report was published, coverage in the popular press was predictable: 'Too Much Sex and Violence, say Teachers'; 'Violence and Smut Dismay Teachers'. These are simplistic encapsulations that we had in fact been careful to avoid. But teachers, as much as parents, are entitled to feel concerned about the medium that dominates children's leisure hours. Perhaps the teachers contributing to the Report were in danger of casting themselves as killjoys, interfering in what was not their business. Yet surely the influence of popular television on children is a legitimate and necessary concern for all of us?

The committee was anxious to avoid the kind of prescriptive conclu-

24

sions which have discredited some previous studies. It did not seek to censor programmes designed for adults. It did express concerns about the way television presents images of the world to young people and relays particular attitudes and values; it suggested ways of keeping those concerns before the public.

Two recommendations emerged:

1. That teachers, parents and broadcasters should find better forums for exploring their understanding of the impact of television on the young and ensuring its impact is not damaging;

2. That, in schools, teachers *in general* should be involved in teaching children to watch television more critically and in equipping them to question the values and assumptions projected by television. Media literacy is a matter for the whole curriculum and should not be seen as a discrete subject.

The first recommendation is the more contentious. Programme-makers are understandably suspicious of do-gooding groups commenting on the content of programmes. Any 'watch committee' seeking to ensure that television projects positive or educational values would, quite rightly, be laughed out of court. Nevertheless, the BBC and the IBA find it worthwhile to organise a significant structure of consultative committees to advise producers on the general as well as the specific content of programmes: agricultural advisory committees, science consultative committees, medical, religious and industrial committees. Their members comment not just on specialist programmes like *Farming Today* or *Medicine Now*, but on the presentation of specialisms right across the output. The educational advisory structure confines itself to educational programmes. Yet youngsters spend more of their time watching general programmes than they do Schools Television or even programmes aimed specifically at children such as *Grange Hill*. Should we not, therefore, be examining how teachers could make more effective contributions to the general deliberations of broadcasters?

It is important to ensure that broadcasters do not feel threatened by such a proposal. The aim must not be to harness their purposes to those of narrow-minded and didactic educators. For their part, the educators must avoid the temptation to tell others what to think.

But the producers and – perhaps more particularly – the schedulers of television surely have responsibilities beyond the narrow ones of technical and aesthetic competence: responsibilities analagous to those responsibilities of teachers that extend beyond the measurable. Teachers are remarkably free of obligations in the classroom, yet their professionalism would be open to question if they were not, within recognised limitations, giving attention to some important considerations. Are teachers offering an interesting and varied programme, seeking to equip students with the tools and desire for further development? Are they using all the resources, both technical and abstract, at their disposal? Is the capacity of each child fully recognised and utilised? Is the curriculum suitable for the whole range of abilities, aptitudes and attitudes within the class and not just for those of the majority? Are the weak protected from the bullies, and the disturbed and disorganised protected from themselves? Are teachers eschewing sarcasm and cruelty? The duty to attempt to operate a code is clear even though there will not always be agreement on the content of the code or the ability to measure the effects of our efforts. This is not to suggest that the producers of *Minder* or the Directors of Programming are in the same business as teachers and timetablers; nor, indeed, that television should ignore the unpleasant, the challenging or even the inane. It is an argument about *professionalism* – not professionalism as a concern with technical competence or the mystique of the craft, but professionalism as the ethical obligations of citizens in a privileged position operating in the affective domain. Many if not most children spend more time each week watching television than they do in the classroom. This suggests that it is incumbent upon broadcasters to consider the impact of individual programmes and of the total output with a professionalism similar to that which informs the activities of teachers.

While this clearly happens in many areas, such as in the provision of minority programmes, drama, science and documentaries, the committee's report indicates that much of the output ignores aspects of reality or reduces it to a one-dimensional simplicity. For children, the images of reality received from popular entertainment programmes are a major part of their information about the world. The Report recommends that 'there should be at the least a clearer recognition among those in television at all levels that just as entertainment should not be missing from that which is primarily educational, education does not stop just because a programme is described as a play, a feature film or light entertainment' (p.114, below).

The committee felt that television establishes stereotypes, reinforces prejudices, sets agendas. The broadcasters may believe they are simply reporting or reflecting the values and nature of society. But it is hard to deny, even though it cannot be proved, that television, like schooling, has a formative effect on popular values. It may be that the harassed producer has ceased to worry about what can neither be measured nor controlled and the pursuit of dramatic journalism and of high ratings is likely to come before considerations of range, depth, balance and subtlety. But the BBC and the IBA do still take their public service role seriously. And it does no harm to repeat that these are issues which concern non-broadcasters who have a right to a say in the matter. It might even be suggested that greater emphasis on professionalism and

26

critical rigour would benefit all viewers and not just the youngsters who are the concern of this essay.

The programme viewing undertaken by the authors of the Report was surprisingly pleasant. Most of the output monitored, from *Top of the Pops* to *World in Action*, was well-made and eminently watchable. If teachers could command the attention of pupils as effectively as television holds viewers they would no doubt be more ambitious in their aims. None the less, it was felt that there was a potential for popular television to be more informative and educational without sacrificing entertainment value. Television, as it were, could do better. . . .

If teachers are asking more of broadcasters, should they not also be asking more of themselves? What can teachers do, for their part, to educate children's responses to television? Media studies has emerged as the focus for teaching children to handle television with sophistication. And here a note of warning is necessary. In mathematics we have faced the problem for many years that ideas or new approaches generated by academics became distorted and transposed as they trickle down to the classroom teacher. On occasions they do more harm than good. Media studies, like psychology or sociology, can present difficulties when attempts are made to simplify the concepts involved so that they become accessible to schoolchildren. It may be that we should be talking in terms not of an academic specialism (Tele-Lit to 'O' Level) but of the responsibility falling on all teachers to help children get the most out of television and, where necessary, to be critical of what they view. Perhaps the media specialists should concentrate first on educating and training teachers, including those who have been in post for many years, and making their message accessible to teachers of varying disciplines.

The question at the heart of this argument is: 'What is Media Studies?' Should media studies be a vehicle for social criticism; a study of advertising to develop an attack on profit and material acquisition; or the use of a war film to editorialise about pacifism? Or should media studies be an attempt to produce a more visually sophisticated audience? At school level the latter must surely come first. It seems likely that society's wider educational aims are best served by a relaxed approach that seeks to encourage teachers to use popular television as a stimulus to discussion for young people in the same way that popular literature has been used for years.

An initiative in training teachers to use television should interest media academics and broadcasters alike. We need to build constructive links with broadcasters going far beyond the end-of-term trip to studios. We need to introduce children to the art and science of production. We need to continue pressure for a relaxation of the copyright restrictions on showing non-educational programmes so that popular television can be brought into the classroom. An increase in visual literacy – the creation of a more critically-aware audience – is a reasonable social and

27

educational aim. It would certainly be of no small benefit to the broadcasters or, at least, to our existing public service broadcasting organisations, as they prepare to face the competition from down-market cable and satellite services.

PART II
BROADCASTERS' PERSPECTIVES

4. HOW CAN BROADCASTERS BE INVOLVED?

MARGARET MATHESON

How can broadcasters not be involved? Going to school and watching television are the two commonest unnatural experiences in life. My ideal is that schools should teach anything their pupils want to learn – the traditional apparatus of curriculum and exams provides an unwelcome limitation to children's abilities to discover what interests them individually. In such a world surely television would feature as an important subject, but like sex it usually seems to be a dirty word.

Television – the presence in family and domestic life that's even more potent than family conversation let alone radio and printed journalism – is ignored or at any rate deemed unfit for study in our schools. It's especially odd now. Television has been in most homes for over twenty years. Battles have been fought and sometimes won to improve the quality and daring of television drama, documentary and news. And there is no sign that children are watching less television than before. Schoolteachers and their charges may very well be able to tell us why. One of the joys of television study is the fact that pupils may have a greater knowledge of current television programmes than their teachers.

How excellent it would be if teachers and children could be engaged in even a modest study, reflectively and with wise consideration, of the one-way speaking picture show that is turned on day and night in the corner of the living room. To start with, the advantages to the children might be found in a more critical and less passive acceptance of all they watch. Indeed it may well be that the study of television produces a generation of viewers who will not watch gormlessly but *search out and see* old and new meanings from what's beamed out.

A new discipline is required, changeable as the awesome changes in television arts, crafts and technology. Let children understand who's paying and why. But to get bogged down teaching the arcane practices of broadcasting bureaucracies and institutions as social science would be as dreary as teaching zoology based upon the administrative niceties of running zoos. And let us not render television impotent by teaching it as we teach art and literature now.

I suspect that television serves to dull children's feelings as well as

31

their perceptions of their own experience more than it excites them. The middle way of indifference probably produces middle minds. Television may well serve to fill those gaps in lives which are empty and frightened of experience. Even if I am wrong in supposing this, then it will be helpful if a study of television shows why. Watching television demands little effort for it is an active agent in the living room asking for passive reaction. It is the guest who relentlessly addresses you. The guest you are free to shut up by turning off. Even so, it remains for the time being unavoidable. It creates and re-creates public events and private episodes. It is hard for a child to remain neutral to what is broadcast day in and out, so perhaps it may be best to start by assisting children to understand for themselves what it is they either hate or like. Why, we might ask for example, does Orson Welles hate television? 'I hate it', he said, 'as much as peanuts. But I can't stop eating peanuts.' So, for starters, if we can't stop watching it, then we and our children deserve the right to know why. If teachers cannot offer a cogent explanation then they should go to work on finding out.

Those of us in broadcasting, whatever our role, ought to encourage the educational agencies to think hard and now about the absence of television study. The search for a discipline of it could well be both noble and revolutionary. Let us start by being idealistic. W. H. Auden said of poetry that it can do 'a hundred and one things, delight, sadden, disturb, amuse, instruct.' There's no earthly reason why a study of television need not try and encourage us, the broadcasters, to try and do the same. 'Imaginative awe' was what Auden said every poem needs to be rooted in. That could be a fine starting point for television study.

The cowardly alternative is to continue to do nothing; to tolerate television as some bastard art or craft concocted by corrupt governments and greedy corporations; to say that it is a fact of society which it's hopeless to do much about, and which we all want to be as harmless as possible; a fact of the century which won't cause trouble so long as committees issue reports and report back to each other, so long as official bums keep seats warm in the boardrooms of our commercial and cultural organisations.

It is the nature of institutions that they are bad at self-criticism, but broadcasting will fossilise without a constant radical critique from its consumers. If we do not assist our children to demand they be served better by television each year, if we do not insist they be served better by television study and television criticism whether in the classroom or the press, then they will, one day, be entirely right to say that we were the ones who allowed television to sink complacently and irretrievably into some uncharted and increasingly sinister bog of mindless drivel. The case for television study is obvious. The educational mandarins must provide the structure for the discipline. Those of us who produce and broadcast the programmes must provide the means and encouragement whenever we are called upon to do so. I hope the call comes soon and that broadcasters answer it with patience and generosity to excite imaginative awe.

5. A ROLE FOR BROADCASTERS

JOHN CAIN

It is surprising to me that the relationship between schooling and television should arise in such a way as to produce the interest and passion it evidently does. Why not the Press and Schooling, the Cinema and Schooling, Radio and Schooling, Magazines and Schooling? Each of these subjects to a greater or lesser degree has had its day and its enthusiastic followers. Why are these connections – between education and the so-called 'mass' media – thought to be important and legitimate concerns of education, and why is television's part thought by many to be the dominant one?

I am not aware that any well-designed research has been done to answer this question. Presumably it is felt that, in contemporary society, the mass media, and television in particular, provide the really significant material which informs and moulds the views of most children; that they are a primary source of news, entertainment and education; and that mass media assumptions, prejudices and influence have therefore to be questioned by teachers. I am not at all sure myself that this is an accurate view but will assume so in what follows, just pausing to observe that experience teaches me that children (and indeed adults) are remarkably resistant to what they do not want to hear or see, that they obtain their 'world view' from a very numerous and diverse set of sources, and that, in any case, the view they get from television is unlikely to be a homogeneous and consistent one other than in a very general sense. It is presumably this 'general' sense which worries media critics.

The first and most obvious way in which broadcasters have been concerned with these questions from the very earliest days of broadcasting is through educational broadcasting. John Reith was insistent that education was one of the chief social functions of broadcasting and the role it played from the early twenties through radio (Schools Radio was 60 years old in 1984) has for nearly 30 years been carried on by television. Much has been written on this subject so I will just content myself with the observation that I believe school (and continuing education) broadcasting has provided and continues to provide schools and colleges with a wide range of excellence in drama, news, current affairs, science, etc., so that educators using the medium responsibly can *bring high-quality material to their classes in the audio-visual mode.* This must surely be regarded as the broadcasters' first responsibility. To see that good plays are performed well, to make the latest science available, to provide authentic French speech, to illuminate history and current affairs, etc. The fact that this material can, under certain conditions, be recorded and used as a semi-permanent resource should not blind us to the fact that the rest of the output is also available for study use but in a much more restricted way. We have to find ways of solving the general copyright issue but that is another very complex question which deserves attention in itself.

Amongst this educational material, and indeed, within general output, we find many programmes which illustrate the second important function broadcasters should in my opinion perform; that of *providing a responsible, critical base for the audio-visual material transmitted* and indeed any other audio-visual material such as film which children are likely to see. For the BBC it can be claimed that year after year programmes are provided for schools and colleges exploring the nature of documentary film, the question of news construction and bias, the way in which drama is made in television, the relevance of film in historical study, the nature and practice of film animation, etc., etc. Independent Television, too, has an honourable record in this field and, between them, the two parts of the British broadcasting duopoly can claim to have provided education with a very substantial body of material directly relevant to media studies; *Scene, Viewpoint, Inside the News, Ways of Seeing, Film as Evidence* are just some titles from the past that spring to mind.

Once we move away from the direct way in which educational broadcasters can serve media studies by providing audio-visual material designed for critical study in the classroom then the question of what else can be done becomes much more difficult to answer with certainty. From a purely practical point of view there is the obvious fact that timetables are already overloaded as new subjects such as media studies, peace studies, women's studies, black studies, third world development studies and trade union studies jostle with the more conventional subjects. This is very controversial ground which it would be imprudent and impractical for me to enter into except to say, first, that the amount of time any school can give to media studies or any other studies on the list above is going to be very limited indeed. Second, and to make the mixture more explosive, one observes that all the subjects mentioned are highly value-laden or, to put it another way, highly contentious. Most BBC and ITV speakers at media studies and research conferences know that many of the texts used in the subject are slanted against the broadcast institution and that a large number of teachers of the subject have what appears to the practising broadcaster to be a very superficial and partial view of the realities of broadcasting.

This is not to say that criticism of broadcasting is unjustified – much of it is sound and should be taken seriously – nor does it mean that television should in some way be shielded from attack and children kept ignorant of the facts. It does mean, however, that what I believe to be a reasonably fair and unbiased view should be presented to children. The trouble is that many critiques of the media are lodged in a philosophy which says this is not possible. So we have an impasse. Broadcasters themselves must share much of the blame when they find themselves in a situation where rather badly researched studies of the media are used as textbooks in the subject. They should be more diligent in writing responses and generally defending what I believe to be a very defensible position. Some would no doubt argue that they have better things to do but this is really not good enough.

There are, then, four points I want to make about what I think media studies should be doing:

1. Questions concerning the political and economic nature of broadcasting institutions are immensely complex ones and should not be answered, especially for children, in terms of crude ideology.

2. If they *are* to be tackled they must have brought to them, in as effective a way as is possible, all the criteria of completeness of information, fairness and accuracy that are demanded by any respectable subject.

3. Since we live in a pluralistic society, this implies the hearing of many viewpoints, including those of people who actually work in the media.

4. That what can be said critically about broadcasting institutions can be said about the press, radio, parliament, the film industry and education (including the organisation and writing of media studies and research sociology!).

My conclusion is that this is a tall order for most schoolchildren and that I would be reasonably content if my own children left school with the critical apparatus necessary to sort out (in a semiological sense) good programmes from bad ones, honest reporting from dishonest reporting, and the various tricks used by advertisers and politicians to induce people to buy shoddy goods and believe in crass policies. In other words, to resist what Orwell referred to, I think, as 'the rattle of the stick in the swill bucket'. In saying this one is asking for no more than what is expected in English, History, Science and Geography.

However, if more is to be attempted, then the standards of scholarship and writing in media research must be improved and broadcasters must accept they have a part to play. Only in this way will media studies be better informed to consistently reach the comprehensiveness found in, say, Masterman,[1] or in Fiske and Hartley.[2] Indeed, even with these authors I have arguments. For example, Masterman in his otherwise excellent bibliography to *Teaching about Television* rather surprisingly excludes 'books and articles written by professional broadcasters themselves', adding in brackets '(though teachers may occasionally find these of value)'. It is not without interest that Masterman does include references to publications originating from inside the BBC and IBA but most are accompanied by somewhat disparaging remarks.

On the other hand critics of these institutions generally get encouragement. Despite its many good qualities, it is a pity a book on teaching should take such a biased line. Its treatment of the ideological role of television, whilst interesting, is particularly tendentious and it is unfortunate that the impression is given that no other view exists.

Alongside the need to provide high-quality material and a critical base against which to judge it, broadcasters must *engage actively with educators and others in the debate about TV and radio and their role in society, providing accurate and comprehensive information on all aspects of the subject from the standpoint of the practitioners.* They may do this through writing, through speaking, by discussions, and through encouraging research, but if they do not do these things then they leave the field wide open to tendentious and ideologically simplistic arguments which are bad scholarship and a disservice to real education.

The work of the Glasgow Media Group[3] which seems to inform some media studies is a case in point. One does not object to polemic, especially if it appears to make some telling points, but polemic dressed as academic research is more difficult to take. The tone of the volumes so far produced is biased and arrogant, the very qualities being attributed to the broadcasters. Yet this very work is being quoted endlessly as if it had some 'scientific' validity.

The mention of research brings me to my last point. For a number of reasons certain kinds of research are viewed with suspicion, probably correctly, by many broadcasters. It is costly, time-consuming, frequently sets out to 'prove' what it already believes and is based on quasi-scientific foundations.

Nevertheless, my personal belief is that we need as much research as we can get on the social effects and implications of the media – a subject more suitable for higher education studies than school studies – and that broadcasters *should encourage research in all the ways they can,* provided it is well designed and executed and does not have the sole function of bolstering some existing prejudice (as distinct from supporting or refuting a well-conceived theory). We cannot, in my opinion, expect research of a very general sociological kind to do more than give us tentative hints which is why it is depressing that much of

37

what is presently published is so sure of itself. But specific and modest small-scale studies have an important cumulative effect in informing media studies. My feeling is that media research and media studies are far too young and immature to stand the burden of 'grand theory' and that much of the grand theory which exists is subjectively overblown. For example, a recent second look at the essays in *Mass Communication and Society*,[4] published only seven years ago, reveals a great deal of airy-nothingness wrapped up in pretty contorted and opaque language. This is not to say that there are no useful contributions in that book – some are excellent – but they tend to be the descriptive, non-theoretical pieces. I am not against theory in media research and studies, but let it be more self-effacing.

Thus I summarise what I believe should be the interests and responsibilities of broadcasters in media education as follows:

1. Provide good quality programmes in all relevant subjects.

2. Provide an informed critical base for audiovisual studies.

3. Get involved in the debate by providing facilities, information, etc.

4. Encourage responsible and well-designed research.

By all these means I hope a continuing and well-ordered debate can develop among teachers, children, parents and broadcasters.

References

1. L. Masterman, *Teaching about Television*, Macmillan, 1980.
2. J. Fiske and J. Hartley, *Reading Television*, Methuen, 1978.
3. Glasgow University Media Group, *Bad News*, Routledge and Kegan Paul, 1976; *More Bad News*, Routledge and Kegan Paul, 1980; *Really Bad News*, Writers and Readers, 1982.
4. J. Curran, M. Gurevitch and J. Woollacott (eds.), *Mass Communication and Society*, Edward Arnold and Open University Press, 1977.

PART III
CRITICAL PERSPECTIVES

6. TAKING POPULAR TELEVISION SERIOUSLY

RICHARD DYER

Two of the most widespread notions used in the discussion of television are 'entertainment' and 'representation'. Both are powerful terms, with a wealth of connotations. We tend to take them for granted, without examining just what is at stake in them. They tend to be kept apart – we talk about either whether a programme is entertaining or how it represents reality to us. Following that habit of mind, I shall begin by discussing each term separately, before suggesting how each is in fact an aspect of the other.

Entertainment
'Entertainment' is a cornerstone of common sense. It is a term we all use, all the time. Like all common sense terms, its meaning is utterly obvious until we come to define exactly what we mean by it. It is only then that we recognise what a difficult concept it is.

The DES Report offers a good instance. The Report recognises that there is a problem about entertainment but it talks about entertainment in characteristic ways that sidestep the question of what entertainment is. The Report either raises the question of whether 'serious' topics should be dealt with in entertainment programmes or else it backs off from its analyses with apologetic remarks about such-and-such being 'only' or 'just' entertainment. In either case, what entertainment is remains unquestioned and unexamined.

What I mean by taking entertainment seriously is asking why and how programmes are entertaining, why people like them and what children's main experiences of television are. These are serious questions because they take us to the heart of the reasons why most people watch television. What I do *not* mean by taking entertainment seriously is looking at popular television programmes, noting that they are entertaining and then saying they are *also* about something Serious and Important. I am not arguing for a line of reasoning like 'Of course we all really enjoyed *Minder* but we also thought that . . .' Rather, I want to understand what the enjoyment is about.

It is customary to come to terms with entertainment in either of two ways. The first is by recourse to a notion of 'escapism'. This is the term used as a full stop to the difficult question of trying to say what is meant about a programme's entertainment quality. In defence of liking *Crossroads* or *Magnum* it is said, 'Oh, well, it's just escapism'. What is rarely asked is what it is we are escaping from and what we are escaping to. To begin to ask this, particularly of producers and children, may help us understand the experience of the pleasure of popular television. As a start, asking people what it was about a programme they enjoyed that offered them escape often reveals even by implication what they wanted to escape from.

Let me take an example from the DES Report of how we may learn from listening to what people say about their enjoyment of entertainment. One of the pupils quoted gives as his reasons for liking *Top of the Pops* that it annoys his father and makes him stop thinking about the problems of the world. These remarks already point to qualities of *Top of the Pops* as entertainment; as a way of offering escape into a world clearly defined as 'youth', with an edge of rebelliousness and cussedness in its liveliness. They suggest a very different experience from that of ageing rockers who moan about *Top of the Pops* being too soft. There are also 'the problems of the world' that *Top of the Pops* implicitly suggests should be escaped from and the busyness, colour, vitality and a certain kind of sexuality that offers an escape from them. By pursuing these lines of reason, then, we can begin to make sense of how *Top of the Pops* and its viewers construct what the problems of the world are and how they can escape from them. Teachers could take these commonsense remarks further. Although one might be cautious about exploring the boy's relations with his father, the family scene is clearly crucial to understanding the dynamics of pleasurable escape into television.

It is important not to confine such discussion to programmes that come already labelled as 'entertainment'. *Tomorrow's World*, which comes on just before *Top of the Pops*, should equally be analysed as entertainment. This does not mean looking at the way it 'sugars the pill' in providing information about technological matters but, rather, looking at the way it constructs its own escape route from the problems of the world. What is entertaining about *Tomorrow's World* is the way that it constructs a tomorrow for today's world to escape into via the unproblematic, colourful, jaunty use of technology. The core of *Tomorrow's World*'s appeal is just as much escapism as *Top of the Pops*.

The other way we can approach entertainment is through a notion that is the opposite of escapism. We get much pleasure from escaping into another world, but we also enjoy having our ideas about the world confirmed. Television entertainment gives us the pleasure of seeing that we are not alone in thinking as we do about the world since it appears others think our way, too. There are perhaps two aspects to this pleasure of confirmation. One is the pleasure of feeling we belong to a consensus.

No consensus arises naturally out of what people just happen to think.

Top of the Pops as entertainment; as a way of offering escape into a world clearly defined as 'youth', with an edge of rebelliousness and cussedness in its liveliness.

What is entertaining about *Tomorrow's World* is the way that it constructs a tomorrow for today's world to escape into via the unproblematic, colourful, jaunty use of technology.

Television is one of many agencies in society that defines what it thinks is the prevailing consensus and then presents it as if it arises spontaneously from what 'people' think. None the less, we do need to acknowledge that there is something very comfortable about a consensus, a feeling of reconciled differences, common ground between people. When watching television it is very pleasant if you can feel that you belong to the consensus it presents.

The other pleasure of confirmation is the opposite. We all of us also recognise that, in certain aspects of our lives, our thoughts and feelings are not those of the consensus we are presented with. We are thus 'deviants' in those aspects. Every so often television may also throw up images and moments that are not within its consensus, and among them one may find one's own 'deviance' confirmed.

Thus on *Question Time* (knockabout entertainment if anything is), one may hear one's own views being expressed. Usually this does not prove them true – no new evidence is offered, there is no leap forward in reasoning – but it is delightful to hear oneself being spoken, legitimised for a fragile second.

To understand entertainment as both escapism and confirmation is not necessarily to endorse it. Television entertainment identifies the problems to be escaped from, how that escape is to be effected and what the consensus and the deviant positions are. All of these issues are of great political consequence, but we have to get at the issues and their consequence through the experience of entertainment, rather than inferring social implications beneath or despite the entertainment, in the characteristic way exemplified by the DES Report

Representation

Turning now to the concept of *representation*, which needs to be discussed in wider terms than the Report allows. We can distinguish four different connotations of the term, each of considerable importance. First, representation suggests re-presentation, presenting reality over again to us. It is often said that television is a 'window on the world', transparent and unmediated; and it is equally often said that it is nothing of the sort, that it is pure fabrication. The notion of representation can get us out of this empty opposition by focusing on the way television actively makes sense of a world that none the less exists separately from television. 'Representation' insists that there is a real world, but that our perception of it is always mediated by television's selection, emphasis and use of technical/aesthetic means to render that world to us.

Equally there is no perception of the world except one that is mediated through the forms of representation available in the culture, of which television is one of the most powerful. The notion of representation keeps open that tension between television images themselves and the reality

44

that those images *make* sense of. What is politically at stake here is *what* sense they make of the world, not the inescapable fact that they do so.

Secondly, 'representation' suggests the function of 'being representative of'. In other words, it raises the question of *typicality*. To what extent are representations of men and women, whites and blacks, different classes, etc. typical of how those groups are in society? All communication must deal in the typical. We cannot communicate only through the utterly unique, particular and individuated. It is unhelpful to fall into the position, as the Report often does, that considers stereotypes as *necessarily* derogatory. What matters is not *that* we have typical representations on television, but rather *what* they are, what harm they do to the well-being of the groups that they represent.

Thirdly, there is representation in the sense implied in the Representation of the People Act, that is, in the sense of *speaking for and on behalf of*. This is where the most political heat is generated because, faced with television images, we constantly need to ask not 'What is this image of?' so much as 'Who is speaking here?'. For every image of a woman, it is important to ask who is speaking for women at that point. In the vast majority of cases, the answer would be a man. The same is true of other groups excluded from the mainstream of speech in our society. Television so often speaks on our behalf without letting us speak for ourselves.

Finally, representation should also make us think of the *audience*. In this inflection, we should include ourselves: what does this programme represent to me; what does it mean to other people who watch it? We often leave this stage out of account; especially, I regret to say, in education. Teachers often try to get pupils and students to see what a programme represents 'ideally' (i.e. as *teachers* understand it) without also finding out what it represents to them. We need to learn to listen better – especially to children – to understand what sense they in turn make out of the work represented to them.

Questions that teachers can debate with their pupils stem readily from these different connotations of the term representation. What sense of the world is this programme making? What does it claim is typical of the world and what deviant? Who is really speaking? For whom? What does it represent to us, and why?

Entertainment and Representation
'Entertainment' and 'representation' are terms kept by convention apart. They even belong to different registers of speech – *entertainment* is a commonsense word, *representation* is far more academic. Along with this goes an assumption that entertainment is not important but trivial, whereas representation is a serious, even heavy issue. Yet we need to look at the way all entertainment necessarily uses representations of the world, just as all representations have, to a greater or lesser extent,

45

entertainment value. We need to be asking why there is an opposition between entertainment and representation. It is common to think of them as in some sense antagonistic functions of television. Some argue that 'this' is a representation of 'that', but it is 'only entertainment' and therefore of no consequence. Alternatively, more perniciously, entertainment is seen to allow the representation to do its work under cover of the pleasure of the programme. We need to get beyond the assumptions contained in such views, to discuss with students the extent to which they feel that the fact that something is entertainment has written off the way it represents the world, and the extent to which they use the entertainment qualities of the programme to defend themselves against its representational concerns. We need to find out about these things and not start by assuming that we already know them.

Even more importantly, we should ask why certain representations are entertaining. Why is this view of reality enjoyable? Why is that view of what social groups are like a pleasure? It may be that given images are entertaining because they represent how we think life should be. If we take the example of images of women, they may represent fantasies of how women should be which may be nice to escape into. They may reassure people who are anxious about changing roles of women, boys who are anxious in their dealings with girls, and girls who reject the new ideas of womanhood that are currently in society. I don't wish to endorse these pleasures, but I do wish to understand the power of images through what makes them pleasurable.

I have been trying to work here from ideas about entertainment and representation that generate questions. Like all the best educational questions, these must be open-ended questions, not ones to which we already have the answers. On the contrary, we need to learn to listen to the answers to the questions; teachers, especially, need to be in a genuine dialogue with their students and pupils. To take popular television seriously is to get inside the experience of it, to grant a legitimacy to the pleasures it offers and *then* to ask questions of value, social responsibility and politics.

7. CHILDREN'S TELEVISION: THE GERMINATION OF IDEOLOGY

BOB FERGUSON

Discussion about the relationships between popular television and schoolchildren tends to concentrate on the potential effects on younger people of popular programmes, usually made for an adult audience. In this framework, most argue – from an effects perspective – that there is a great deal to worry about. There are other approaches, however, which contradict many of the assumptions here and set up a different framework. For teachers engaged in media studies, for instance, there is a greater concern to come to terms with the various elements that compose the genres and structures of popular television's endless discourse.

It is through this second approach that I want to return to the issue of television's effects, since it is important to thoroughly ground assessments of effect in the forms, mediations, intended purposes and possible significance of television. The effects perspective gives little weight to this and so doubt must be cast upon the validity of its conclusions.

I intend to concern myself with programmes specifically made for children. Although I wish to include programmes officially designated as educational, my main concern is with general output programmes for children. My purpose is polemical: to suggest that there is at least as much to be concerned about in the representations offered to a child audience as in the representations offered to adults but watched by children. Debate about effects has to move beyond the moral panics which are often generated over the important issue of representations of sex and violence. The terrain upon which to engage with programmes made for children will be intellectual, political, ideological. It will involve teachers in recognising the urgency of teaching about modes of representation just as much as the explicit and implicit discourses which can be identified in programmes for children.

The reason why this is important and urgent is that there is a danger that programmes made for children can inhibit their capacity for thought and intellectual development. In order to account for this view, I wish to start from a theoretical notion developed by Herbert Marcuse. It is concerned with what he terms 'the closing of the universe of discourse and action'. For Marcuse, 'ideas, aspirations and objectives that, by their content, transcend the established universe of discourse and action are either repelled or reduced to terms of this universe.'[1]

A developed notion of discourse is crucially relevant to understand the mode of operation of children's television. Discourse has to be understand as a set of informing principles which permeates the construction and articulation of media messages. It is seldom direct in identifying its own origins, but rather works to efface or naturalise itself. This is the ideological function of discourse. It is through discourse that highly specific modes of conceptualising the world are made to seem general or universal. Much of this generality is attained by offering an apparent plurality of messages within children's television. The plurality *is* only apparent because differing views or constructions of the world are always presented from within the framework of the dominant discourse. There is never any chance for the viewer to discover alternative discourses by watching television. The most that s/he may do is to develop, consciously or otherwise, skills of decoding and analysing the dominant discourse. By this operation, a variety of possibilities for people to take action for change are consistently refused.

The established universe of discourse of children's television may be characterised as Anglo-centric, often racist, sexist, royalist, pro-capitalist, ostensibly Christian and as generally arguing that the best way to deal with social problems is through benevolence. Hence the emphasis on raising money through charity for usually worthy causes without questioning why charity has to be invoked instead of direct government action, and the preference for connecting worthy causes to royal patrons rather than to figures in the trades union movement who are struggling against injustice. Charity is noble, struggle is impolite. Multi-culturalism may be just acceptable; anti-racism is coarse and wrongly-motivated.

This is, of course, the established universe of discourse of programmes such as *Blue Peter*. It is also the discourse of programmes for adults and for families. The discourses constructed through individual personalities such as disc-jockey celebrities like Terry Wogan, Jimmy Young and Jimmy Saville are also remarkably similar. It is, however, through children's television that the groundwork is laid for the ideological development so necessary to produce audiences for the vacuous and the reactionary.

The dominant discourse of children's television works to produce future citizens who are well-socialised and the majority of child viewers ingest the discourse unquestioningly. It may be that children pass through phases of watching specific programmes until they reject them as being babyish, but this does not mean that they have thereby refused the informing principles of those discourses. They have merely been placed on the ideological shelf for future use. During a period of international tension – such as the Falklands/Malvinas conflict or a

48

Royal pregnancy – they will be taken down, dusted off and used with varying degrees of intensity.

The television coverage of the Falklands/Malvinas conflict is a case in point. Its effects are not necessarily direct – on consciousness and behaviour – but are certainly indirect – on consensual attitudes 'naturally' held. So, although the viewer may have rejected a possible career in the armed forces, this would not stop her/him from believing that the British armed forces are the best in the world, nor that it is better to be British than Latin American, nor that the Union Jack (the last, gaudy signifier of an Empire best forgotten) is the symbol of 'what it means to be British'. Flag-waving is an ideological disease which the purveyors of the dominant discourse love to parade before mass audiences at every opportunity.

There are, of course, certain young people who do reject the values implicit in the discourse of children's television. But their rebellion is often short-lived. The pull towards ideological containment via the smile of Terry Wogan or the inanity of many of the presenters of *Top of the Pops* is very strong. The producers and presenters of programmes such as *Blue Peter* fulfil a function akin to that of the Jesuit educator in preparing the young for their dubious role of viewers with no critical consciousness. With the Jesuits, critical consciousness is a vital factor. For the broadcasters, it has never been on the agenda.

One of the clearest examples of the way in which children's television can close off the universe of discourse can be demonstrated through a closer look at *Blue Peter*. In 1983 the BBC published its twentieth book springing from the *Blue Peter* series. It was designed to celebrate twenty-five years of the programme and was devised and written by Biddy Baxter and Edward Barnes. They explain the origin of the programme:

In 1958, no one ever thought *Blue Peter* would last longer than six or eight weeks. The Head of Children's Programmes for the BBC TV asked one of his producers, John Hunter Blair, to devise a programme that would fill fifteen minutes once a week. John had a think. His great passion was model railways – especially 00 gauge – and he knew girls were keen on dolls, so he asked a blonde beauty queen called Leila Williams, who'd just won the title 'Miss Great Britain 1957', to show the dolls, and an actor called Christopher Trace to run trains on a layout in the studio.[2]

In this condensed history, there is no hint of the vaguest notion of critical consciousness. It reads as a parody designed to create outrageous stereotypes, including a stereotype of a BBC Producer. But it is not a parody. It is as urgently real as the stereotypes it set up in the first programme. The book is written twenty-five years later and the writers are celebrating the institutionalisation of the crassest sexism without turning a hair. It is, for them, both normal and quite acceptable to let this go by without any comment. They are celebrating one of the discourses of children's television. A discourse with the power to define the world and our place in it by naturalising that which is a social construct. They are like the journalist described by Barthes[3] who starts with a concept and seeks a form for it. Boys are boys. Girls are girls. One likes trains and the other likes dolls. The form of *Blue Peter* does the rest. And it is a cumulative, organic form of discourse which, once established, develops a life and a power of its own.

It would be unkind to suggest that *Blue Peter* is the only or main perpetrator of a closed universe of discourse. Jimmy Saville also helps to fix it, as does John Craven, Lassie and The Incredible Hulk. Such mediators as these are constructed through scriptwriters and production teams who 'know' what children need. They manufacture a preferred set of meanings in symbiotic relationship with their stars, be they human or canine. A window on the world is constantly, unproblematically reassembled with an enormous propensity for assimilating the unusual or outrageous and making it visible in terms acceptable to the established universe of discourse. Once drawn into this gentle but compelling vortex of meaning-making, there is little hope of escape. Sid Vicious did it once or twice, but only at the cost of alienating the very people who should have been listening to what he had to say. It would seem to be a closed circle.

But there are other ways of conceptualising and representing the world than the (sometimes necessary) act of raising two fingers at it. It is to these possibilities that I now wish to turn, particularly in relation to the role of the broadcasters who are concerned with making programmes for children. The first point to make is that alternative ways of conceptualising the world should not be confused with showing various points of view on television. A plurality of viewpoints reduced to the terms of a single discourse merely strengthens that discourse. Broadcasters have to be convinced by democratic pressure that there are other ways of conceptualising and articulating media messages than those with which they have undoubtedly been equipped. They have to recognise that they are the vectors of ideology. In this they are no different from broadcasters anywhere else – with one significant exception. In this country they tend to be either unaware or willing to deny the significant role they play. For them, ideology is something which other people have. *They* tend to come from, to use a well-known media phrase, behind the 'so-called' Iron Curtain. *We* are pure, untained, balanced, fair-minded.

To recognise that this argument is a nonsense is a beginning. To be prepared to step into the frameworks of other discourses would be a move towards genuine plurality. We might then be able to view 'Red

50

Boys are boys. Girls are girls. One likes trains and the other likes dolls. The form of *Blue Peter* does the rest.

Peter' every other week. It would be a programme presented, possibly, by two women and one man. It would campaign against any government that could tolerate poverty, degradation, poor housing or health care. It would be openly anti-royalist, anti-racist and anti-sexist. It would deplore the need for charity when millions of pounds are spent each minute to defend us from a future. If funds were raised, they would be for publicity campaigns against nuclear arms and against pusillanimity in the face of privilege.

Any broadcasters reading this may have already decided that they are reading the words of an ideologically-warped person. Yet it has to be noted that there are many women and men, black and white, who would welcome such a programme as the one I have just outlined. And their children, if they have any, would probably welcome it even more.

The point I am making is, of course, polemical. But it *is* serious. Until broadcasters are willing to recognise that the world might be other than it is and that they and their viewers might be involved in the process of change, they will be exercising only their power of complacency. And it is through the discourses of children's television that we are also able to witness the complacency of ideological power.

There is a case for broadcasters, parents and teachers getting together to discuss these issues. It is time.

References

1. H. Marcuse, *One Dimensional Man*, Abacus, 1972, p.24.
2. B. Baxter and E. Barnes, *Blue Peter Book 20*, Scholastic Publications, 1983, p.6.
3. R. Barthes, *Mythologies*, Paladin, 1976, p.128.

8. ON THE OFFENSIVE: TELEVISION AND VALUES

JOHN CAUGHIE

Whatever is published is presumed to be in some way approved, or at least condoned, by the society which permits its publication. Every programme reflects the standards of decency and acceptability which are held, not only by the producer and his professional colleagues and superiors in the hierarchy, but also by the broadcasting audience. . . . In the theatre, cinema or bookshop you pay and thereby choose to see or read what is there. In television you make no such choice; and it is not a rebuttal to say that the viewer can press the button and change the channel after he has been grossly offended. The viewer feels himself implicated in the offensive act.

(Annan Committee Report on the Future of Broadcasting, HMSO, March 1977, p.246)

There is a problem around the question of the offensive in thinking and teaching about television. It seems always to be assumed that the offence is directed against a set of values which have been generally and finally agreed. It is the consensus which is offended. What I want to do here is to contest the assumption of consensual values and rework (in a sense, reappropriate) the notion of the offensive.

In rejecting the rhetoric of consensus which characterises the Annan Report – a discourse whose official male pronoun is almost poignantly symptomatic of an assumption of a homogeneous society in which audiences, producers and hierarchies are held together in a celestial harmony of commonly held standards of decency and acceptability – in rejecting that, do I also have to forget or consign to insignificance the anger which I quite commonly feel at the routine offensive acts of representation which television casually naturalises? Is there a way of talking about that anger – which does indeed have to do with being implicated, with being the passive object of an assumption about who I am, or about who we are as very various and fractionalised audiences – without lending support to the militant discourse of the National Viewers and Listeners Association? A large part of the problem is that the terrain around the question of value and values, of the good, the bad and the offensive, has been evacuated; a vacant property for the NVALA to squat in under the authority of the moral consensus.

The evacuation seemed like a good idea at the time. In trying to separate itself from the establishment of literary criticism, post-1968 film theory (and a substantial part of literary theory also) challenged the obsession with the author and with his or her place on an apparently agreed scale of greatness within the cultural tradition. Semiotics, structuralism and post-structuralism gave very little, if any, place to evaluation as a critical objective, and sought instead other kinds of knowledge about how texts worked. But more than that, for film and television evaluative criticism had always worked against the popular. The popular was simply that which fell off the bottom of the ladder of literary values and dropped into the lower depths of the merely sociological.

For the serious study of film and television, if the popular were to be established as an area of real cultural concern, the terms of evaluative criticism – 'profundity', 'originality', 'genius' – seemed to be of little help. Evaluative criticism was the enemy of popular culture, and for many of the critics and teachers for whom the late sixties and the seventies were the formative period (myself included) evaluation became a dirty word, and the question of value and values was proscribed.

Now, in no way is this meant to be an act of contrition or ritual recantation. It was absolutely necessary to challenge the methods and assumptions of evaluative criticism, whether its evaluations were explicit or, as is more commonly the case, implicit, and the challenge was, and continues to be, enormously productive. Emphatically, there is no question of a return to a lost true path. It is still not clear to me that evaluation should ever be a primary object of criticism, or that education should be about the cultivation and inculcation of received values. But if the space has been left vacant, undefined and uncontested, it can hardly be a surprise if others take it over and turn it into a very powerful and well-fortified position. The success of the NVALA, and, more pervasively, of the 'moral consensus' position, has been to win a proprietorial authority over the terms of value and offensiveness in such a way that it is very difficult for anyone else to attack the strident certainties of that discourse without being sucked into an accidental defence of the natural right of television and film to produce and circulate oppressive representations. If there is a point to reopening questions of value and values it would be to redefine the terms, and, importantly, to find ways of contesting and resisting certain representations without falling into the automatic language of moral censorship or the appeal to the fiction of common standards of taste and decency.

This seems particularly important for education. The absence of some detailed, hard-edged confrontation with assumptions about value creates an absence at the centre of the teaching of television which makes it very uncertain what that teaching is really about. Is it really just another subject on the curriculum? Is it really just about appreciation? The uncertainty seems to run in two directions. On the negative side, there is control and inoculation; 'The vast majority of young people's viewing,' says the DES Report, 'takes place at home and this lays considerable responsibility on parents to control the amount and nature of the viewing, and to discuss what young people have seen.'[1]

That is to say, if they slip through the controls, discuss it. The assumption is that television, or too much television, or too much popular television, is bad for you. Where authority fails, the liberal panacea of discussion and education can be administered to immunise against the harmful effects. There is, of course, a strong argument for exposing students to a diversity of cultural forms, but where that diversity is reduced to a hierarchy and the object of teaching is, consciously or unconsciously, to lead students up the ladder towards approved culture, replacing cultural heterodoxy with cultural ortho-doxy, then the effect on television teaching is almost entirely negative.

On the more positive side of the uncertainty, television can be viewed not as a threat to approved culture and values but as a rich repository of topics, issues and themes which can be plundered for classroom discussion. The television set becomes an audio-visual aid for social or moral education, continually throwing up Burning Issues, injecting contemporaneity and a sense of engagement into the routines of education.

It is too easy to caricature these two approaches, thereby obscuring some difficulties. Within certain classroom practices it is perfectly legitimate to use television as a source of contemporaneity, and, while control and inoculation may be not only negative but also naive, it is also important to recognise that the line between 'exposing students to a diversity of cultural forms' and 'imposing (unconsciously) my own view of culture' is an extremely thin one indeed. What is really at stake, however, is that, while the negative side of the uncertainty is teaching against television and the positive side is using television to teach, neither side is actually teaching television. In the heat of the chase after values, television is allowed to escape.

To teach about television and social values, which is surely at least one of the things that should be taught about, we have to recognise that the values cannot simply be read off from the television set as if it were a neutral relay, a window through which we can look and see the world in action. And if we are talking about offensiveness, we not only have to recognise that society is much more complex and contradictory in its organisation than is allowed for in a consensus view, we also have to recognise that television is read in quite different ways by quite different audiences. Really to teach about television is to teach about representa-tions, about ways of reading images, about audiences, and about the ways in which television relates to other institutions of culture and of

55

the State. This may seem like a rather daunting list of demands, but they can clearly be approached and taught in a number of ways at a number of levels. What is important is that all of these questions are intricately linked with the question of television's values. To state the obvious, values don't drop to us out of the sky, nor are they simply inherited. They are continually produced and transformed by representations, which are, in their turn, produced and transformed by institutions which operate under institutional, legal, economic and cultural constraints; and these representations are read by viewers and audiences who also operate within constraints and conditions. Merely to study television as an object seems academic (in its more formalist sense). What the study of television offers is one specific way (there are others but television is peculiarly immediate) of understanding how values and representations are produced and transformêd and read.

What I am trying to do is to displace some of the assumptions about the relationship between an audience and television – a homogeneous audience and an abstract television – which seem to stand in the way of a clear understanding of the relationship between television and values by reinforcing the fiction of a moral consensus. What I want to do now is to offer some notes about the difficulties which are lurking in three of the most common abstractions and homogeneities about television and audiences; difficulties which have to be part of thinking about teaching television.

1. Television itself
The difficulty of the notion of 'television itself' can be illustrated by referring to the conference at which the earlier version of this paper was given. It was part of the success of the conference that it followed up the initiative of the DES Report by bringing together teachers and broadcasters to discuss the issue of popular television and schooling. Clearly, the bringing together of these two interested parties, both of whom are again represented in this publication, is extremely important (even if it was a large and vocal majority of teachers and a small and relatively silent minority of broadcasters). But they do represent two distinct constituencies, separate in their interests and in their responsibilities.

For teaching, I would want to argue that television, and the question of value and values on television, cannot be adequately understood by a concentration on individual programmes, or even by a concentration on individual programme categories; popular television, soap opera, news, 'serious' drama. It can only be understood by attending to the forms, practices and routines of television as a whole: those procedures of production and programming which become naturalised within the institution as 'good practice' and appear on the screen as 'good television'. In order to understand the individual bits of television, in other words, it's necessary to understand television itself.

56

To argue this with the broadcasters, however, is to risk letting them slip off the hook. If the problem of television's representations is simply 'television itself', its constraints and conditions, then nobody is responsible and there is nothing to be done. If I am angered or oppressed or offended by a representation of class or sexuality or nationality, I can only blame 'television itself', reconfirm my left-wing melancholia, and leave a space for Mary Whitehouse to claim that she is speaking for me.

Politically, it seems very important to resist the sense of pessimism and inevitability which is contained in the idea of 'television itself': television as a monolithic abstraction, generating representations and values from no identifiable base, staffed by shadows. The difficulty that I want to point to lies in the need to find a position between the educational demand that people should be educated about the procedures and constraints of television, and the political demand that we should hold on to the belief that the forms and representations of television are not natural or inevitable, and that certain bits of television, some of its assumptions about who we are, have to be resisted and can be changed.

2. The Audience

The question which the original of this paper was asked to address was, 'What is regular television watching like?'. In most senses, the question is an impossible one – which is not to say that it is not a useful one. It is not just that I don't watch television very regularly; rather that, even if I did, I wouldn't know what it was like to watch it as a woman, as a black person, or even as an English person. There is no definitive way of watching television regularly. This is not a routine point. Teachers have to recognise that it is really quite difficult to understand, from the perspective and experience of someone born before 1950, the place that television occupies in the experience and cultural formation of someone born after 1970. Even within the category of people born after 1970, it is still very doubtful that there is a useful unified category, 'schoolchildren', any more than there is a category 'audience' or 'society'.

The notion of 'an audience', like the notion of 'television itself', is too general, homogeneous and monolithic. Broadcasters and official reports cling to it as a necessary fiction which supports the consensus; but it is more and more apparently a fiction, constantly contradicted by the refusal and simple inability of many of the fractions of society – fractions of class, sexuality, race, region, nation – to be effortlessly subsumed into a unified national identity of common standards and aspirations. And these fractions of the audience, or, more exactly, these fractionalised audiences, are likely to experience television and its representations in different ways. A miner is likely to experience the news differently from an academic, a woman academic is likely to experience *The Benny Hill*

Show in a different way than a male miner. Even to use these categories is already to hold out hostages to fortune and to make unacceptable assumptions along the lines of received stereotypes. The point is, though, that the idea of television as a monolith effortlessly pumping out a flow of unified and unifying messages to a national audience has to be continually qualified, both by reference to television and by reference to social audiences and social readings. Undermining assumptions about 'the audience' is not to say that questions of audiences aren't crucially important, but they are so in two distinct senses:

a) Television programmes can be studied to detect the ways in which they seek to construct for themselves a national audience, how their rhetoric and address seek to organise an audience. This is a study less of the explicit content of programmes, than of the routines of presentation, language, visual style and editing which assume a particular form of relationship between addresser and addressee: the inclusive and incorporative 'we' of presenters, for instance, or the significance of Frank Bough's pullover.

b) Audiences can be studied, by interview and questionnaire, in their various fractions and categories. The work of David Morley and of Charlotte Brunsdon on *Nationwide*, and Dorothy Hobson's work on *Crossroads* are important contributions in this area.[2]

The first is a study of television representations, but audiences can't unproblematically be read off from it since they are constructed as much by social experiences and by their specific conditions of viewing as by the rhetoric of television. The second is a study of the audience, which may not tell us a great deal about the routine practices and terms of address of television representations. The two can very fruitfully be brought together – in fact it is increasingly doubtful that they can be held apart – but they are not the same thing, and the one can't simply be used to guarantee or refute the other.

Within the practicalities of classroom teaching it may be easier to study in a disciplined way the forms of address which television programmes adopt towards their audiences than it is to do a sociological survey of audience responses (though the classroom poll is a staple device). But that study of address has to be constantly complicated by reminders of difference – different conditions, different audiences, different readings – if the fiction of the homogeneous national audience isn't simply to be replaced by another fiction: the fiction of passive viewers, obedient to address, jumping into line at the call of discourse.

3. Forms of attention
Referring to BARB ratings as a measure of popularity, the authors of the DES Report make the point that 'this method makes no assessment of

A miner is likely to experience the news differently from an academic . . .

. . . a woman academic is likely to experience *The Benny Hill Show* in a different way than a male miner.

59

the amount of attention given to a television programme by members of its audience, and the figures should therefore be treated with caution.'[3] The qualification is an important one and should be extended to the forms of attention which audiences give to programmes as well as to the amount.

Approaching the question again, 'What is regular television watching like?', one very confident response was given by Raymond Williams in his book, *Television: Technology and Cultural Form.* 'In all developed broadcasting systems,' he says, 'the characteristic organisation, and therefore the characteristic experience, is one of sequence or flow.'[4] Williams' concept of 'flow' refers to the fact that to watch television is not to watch a single coherent event in a place set apart from day-to-day living, but is to experience a sequence of events, to move in and out of actuality, fiction, entertainment, education, and in and out of the real world of domestic life and the real world of television. Unlike theatre or cinema or reading which offer discrete events or specific items, on television, says Williams, 'the real programme that is offered is a *sequence* or set of alternative sequences . . ., which are then available in a single dimension and in a single operation.'[5]

The concept of 'flow' has dominated thinking and teaching about television for the last ten years. Usefully, it insists that it is not enough to look at individual segments of the sequence in isolation; their place within the sequence is also determinant. 'Flow' is specific to broadcasting. It is, in fact, one of the very few specific theoretical terms which broadcasting has introduced. But, like 'television itself' and 'the audience', it also lacks differentiation; it too could be examined at closer quarters, at a higher level of magnification.

Briefly, here, I simply want to suggest that while scheduling undoubtedly encourages flow, in order, precisely, to channel the viewer through the evening, nevertheless it is not simply one damn thing after the other, but operates as a hierarchy, certain elements being privileged over other elements. Crucially the top of the hierarchy confers a prestige and a credibility on television as a whole. It is this hierarchy of prestige which has given the single play its status: disproportionately expensive in relation to its audience appeal, it nevertheless establishes television within culture. More generally, the importance of programmes like *Panorama, The South Bank Show, The Jewel in the Crown,* and most of Channel Four isn't simply to do with what they themselves say or do, but has to do also with the cultural 'seriousness' and the credibility which they confer on other parts of television. A controversial play may be uncomfortable for the institution, but it makes television serious.

The concept of flow as a sequence, then, has to be held against the concept of television as a mosaic of interlocking parts, a system of hierarchies in which the various parts are interdependent. The hierarchies within television programming are also interrelated to hier-

60

archies within the wider culture. To assume a uniformity of attention across all these hierarchies would be to assume a quite straightforward correlation between the numbers of people watching a programme and that programme's importance and cultural weight. I would want to argue that audiences watch single plays or *Panorama* in different ways than the same audiences watch, say, *Crossroads*, and that the specific forms of attention which are given to programmes complicates the equation between numbers and cultural or social importance. While some segments of television's flow take their significance from *how many* people watch them, other segments take their importance from *how* people watch them.

There is a point to be made here about the relationship between 'popular' television and 'serious' television. I would argue that different forms of attention are involved, and that these forms of attention are determined by presentation and address, but also by the way programmes are placed within the evening's viewing and within domestic activity. I would not argue that one form of attention is somehow necessarily better, more desirable, more valuable than another.

Clearly, there is a very traditional kind of value judgment involved in the separation of the 'serious' and the 'popular' which follows the line of 'approved culture' and 'unapproved' or 'disapproved' or 'non-' culture. Within education and cultural training it is very often the 'popular' which is to be controlled and inoculated against, while the 'serious' is taken to be thought-provoking and hence valuable. To indicate the difficulty of that I want to refer to a television play/film by David Hare, *Licking Hitler*, which is one of the very few television plays in distribution and becomes educationally important because of that. In the course of the play, which is set during the war, a young, middle-class English woman from an extremely sheltered background is quite brutally raped by a very drunk, boorish and obsessive Scotsman. It's obviously not fair to take events out of their context in the play, but it is the central event: a relationship is established on the basis of the rape, she learns from the experience and eventually sees through her class position. We are being offered symbolic rape within a privileged televisual form: the single play. It is presented as being acceptable because it is symbolic, and because it is the statement of a serious artist. The form of attention which is invited is one which can contemplate rape as an abstraction, a way of representing the penetration of a class and cultural impasse. It is, in other words, an aggressively and exclusively male form of attention. But not only that, it also seems very likely to me that the sexual offence wearing symbolic clothing and disguised as art may circulate in a much more pernicious and dangerous way than, say, the excesses of Kenny Everett, who *could* be argued (I don't think I would argue it) to invite a subversive form of attention by the very excessiveness of his crude sexism.

61

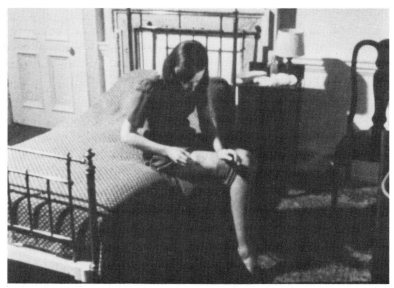

Licking Hitler . . . the sexual offence wearing symbolic clothing and disguised as art.

Kenny Everett . . . invite[s] a subversive form of attention by the very excessiveness of his crude sexism.

This is not a defence of the 'popular' against the 'serious': in terms of representations and values, one can be as oppressive or as progressive as the other. The form of attention which the single play invites can be at least as seductive as the relaxation of popular entertainment; popular forms can be as unpredictable as the single play. While there is a place in the teaching of television for an understanding of the ways in which the terms 'popular' and 'serious' are used within a system of hierarchies of privilege and prestige, there is no place for a separation, based on assumptions of value, which validates one and denigrates the other, or which finds health in one and moral threat in the other.

Which brings me back to the question of value. The motivation for these detours through the generalities of television is to undermine the moral panic about television, a panic which is generated and supported by a desire to go directly to values without passing through television on the way. Television is taken for granted, a channel through which values flow. To understand the relationship between television and social values requires understanding the relationship between television and its audiences; and to do that we have to think about the specific ways in which representations are produced on television and the ways in which they circulate.

What I have tried to do is to break down some of the monolithic generalities which very often get in the way of thinking and teaching about television. But simply to leave them broken down is a recognisably academic strategy which only ensures that debate goes on and on. What I want to do now, in conclusion, is to look again at the question of values.

Throughout, I have tended to hold the two terms, value and values, together, as if they were the same thing. They are not, and it seems necessary now to separate them out a little. Value, within traditional criticism, can involve nothing more than an aesthetic judgement; values seem always to touch on the social and/or the moral. The debate between the social and the aesthetic in criticism has a very long history, but for many of us it takes a particularly confusing form at present. Informed by a tradition of criticism which developed in the sixties around semiotics, structuralism and psychoanalysis, we have come to recognise that values cannot simply be read off texts or found in their contents, but are inscribed in their form of address, in narrative, in the conventions of realism, and they are often inscribed in contradictory ways which can only be properly opened out by precise attention to textual processes. On the other hand, informed by a recognition of what are called 'new social forces' – feminism, in particular, but also other sexual groupings, ethnic groupings and forces of national development – we have come to recognise that values are not simply the abstractions of truth and beauty, but that they take quite material social forms in struggles against oppression and for self-definition. Their concrete

63

Blankety Blank fills a slot . . .

. . . *Widows* occupies a slot, the 9 p.m.-Wednesday-ITV-crime series slot, but transforms it.

urgency cannot always wait for correct formal analysis. But, at the same time, without disciplined analysis, how do we know how the values work? People are oppressed in quite material ways by values and representations which perpetuate their subordination, but how do we inscribe that materiality and that urgency into our criticism and our teaching in ways which don't merely reproduce the simplifications and the self-evident certainties of NVALA? How do we inscribe these material social values into our sense of aesthetic value? These seem to me to be important questions, which the evacuation of the terrain of value, values, discrimination and the offensive have elided. The additional difficulty or confusion (or dithering) for many of us is that we want to make a commitment to the values that, say, feminism struggles for while at the same time protecting our pleasures from the rigours of its demands.

Aesthetically, it seems quite possible to make discriminations. Television, endlessly producing images and programmes and representations, demands repetition. It seems possible to discriminate between certain programmes which only satisfy this ruthless demand for repetition and others which occupy a position of difference. *Blankety Blank* fills a slot. *Widows* occupies a slot, the 9 p.m.-Wednesday-ITV-crime series slot, but transforms it. This is not a distinction related to any straightforward way to a universal aesthetic pleasure since for much of television and much of the audience it is precisely the guarantee of repetition and continuity that produces pleasure. Nor is it a distinction between the 'popular' and the 'serious' since the single play is as likely to do what is expected of single plays as is *Blankety Blank* to repeat the formula of the quiz show. All that the distinction does is to identify a certain kind of pantheon, a particular kind of 'good television'. Since notions of the good very easily creep into teaching, informing choices and evaluations, it is as well to have some sense of the criterion which may be involved.

But faced with the moral consensus, with the militancy of the NVALA, and with the return to Victorian values, it seems educationally and politically less important that we should find a way of establishing the good, and more important that we should find a way of dealing with the bad. By 'bad' I mean the oppressive and the exploitative. It seems important to define a space which has not already been colonised by the strident discourse of moralism from which it is possible to say that some forms of representation should be supported against other forms of representation, some images against other images, and that some programmes and some representations are indeed offensive: offensive in the military sense of 'aggressive', 'threatening', 'an invasion'; offensive also, not necessarily to an assumed consensus of common standards, but to specific defined fractions of the television audience.

Ultimately, if we are concerned with offensiveness and with the

65

possible dangers which television may pose to the social formation and values of young people, we may have to make the leap from a pure aesthetic judgment to a social judgment, and we may have to teach, in whatever form, about social power. This is not to say that we have to go back to using television to teach something else. What we are doing when we teach in this way is to investigate in precise, specific and interrogative ways the forms in which television reproduces, inflects and recirculates in its representations relations of power which are there already in society. What we are teaching is the way in which representations work on and in society. To go back to Kenny Everett: what we are doing if we teach *The Kenny Everett Show* is not simply proscribing it or controlling it; we can use it to show how it reproduces in another form representations of women which are sanctioned elsewhere on television (*Licking Hitler*), elsewhere in the media (Page Three or the Pirelli calendar in the *Sunday Times* Colour Supplement) and elsewhere in social behaviour.

In the end, it does seem to be an important part of teaching television to show its relationship with social relations and social values. Education becomes extensive rather than intensive, moving out from television but without ever leaving television behind or using it as an inert stepping stone to something more important. '. . . If you want to use television for teaching something,' says Umberto Eco, 'you have first to teach somebody to use television.'[6]

References

1. See p.115 below.
2. See Charlotte Brunsdon and David Morley, *'Everyday Television: 'Nationwide'*, BFI Television Monograph 10, 1978; David Morley, *The 'Nationwide' Audience*, BFI Television Monograph 11, 1980; Dorothy Hobson, *'Crossroads': The Drama of a Soap Opera*, Methuen, 1982.
3. See p.97 below.
4. Raymond Williams, *Television: Technology and Cultural Form*, Fontana, 1974, p.86.
5. Ibid, p.87.
6. Umberto Eco, 'Can Television Teach?', *Screen Education* 31, Summer 1979, p.15.

PART IV
TELEVISION, THE MEDIA AND EDUCATION

9. TELEVISION, MEDIA STUDIES AND SCHOOLING

TANA WOLLEN

Do we wish to teach the child, even if we could, to reason theoretically about the production of goods and the performance of services by other people, or do we not rather wish to teach him first, in practice and in the concrete, to produce goods and services himself?

(Lord Eustace Percy, Minister of Education, 1927, quoted in John White, et al, *No, Minister – A Critique of the DES paper 'The School Curriculum'*, University of London Institute of Education, 1981.)

The common concern with popular television should not deflect attention from the fact that television is but one aspect of the media, albeit the most significant. It is important to see newspapers and magazines, films, radio and television as distinct forms of popular culture but also as *industries* sharing similar ideological and economic currency. *Popular TV & Schoolchildren* is itself a case in point. Although it was about television's representations and their effects, it was not television but the newspapers which led the report on the Report.

Television is one medium, then, among the many to offer objects for study within the education system under the title *Media Studies*. It is a relation between Television and Schooling posed by Media Studies that I want to argue for here.

Unequal Relations
It is hard at first sight to see similarities between the media and the education system. Education is a serious and compulsory business. You have to go to school to get taught. You work as a student at school in order to be able to get paid for working in the 'real' adult world of jobs. The media, on the other hand, are involved in that part of our lives devoted to leisure, where nothing is compulsory, where we can choose to engage in activities which we enjoy. Leisure is what we do when we are not at school or at work; having paid for life's essentials, leisure is what most of us work for to enjoy the better. It is these traditional distinctions which often make it difficult to take any media artefact into the classroom and *work* on it. But the boundaries between the media and

69

schooling can be usefully crossed.

The most obvious similarity between them is the fact that in Britain everyone experiences both of them. Almost everyone reads a newspaper, watches TV and listens to the radio. Everyone has some form of schooling. Both the media and schooling educate and inform, albeit in different ways. Both then are principal *socialising agencies* and both agencies are accountable to the public. Broadcasting agencies are sensitive to the reactions of those who consume their products and schools are expected to serve the needs of their students and their communities. Both the media and schools are under the watchdog eyes of government agencies. There are inspectors, government working parties, Education Acts, Broadcasting Acts, White Papers, Green Papers, Reports, etc.

If the media and schooling are not as different as at first sight, what significance can be drawn from the similarities? Since they are experienced by everybody and are directly or indirectly accountable to public demand or government decree, the ways in which the media and schooling function, are administered and organised, need to be learned about. Knowledge of this kind seems to me to be part of the basic equipment required by any citizen living in a democratic society.

More emphatically, because the media and schools together are our main sources of information, education and entertainment, they ought not to be regarded without careful or critical examination. There is a tendency to teach about the media as agencies 'out there' – corrupting the purification processes supposedly at work in schools – rather than as agencies similar to the informing and educating agencies of schooling. Teaching about the media should also make explicit the processes through which people are informed and educated. That is to say, teachers should also be teaching about what they are very much involved in and committed to – the processes of education at work in our own schools and colleges.

Education has generally disapproved of The Media. Children spend too much time watching telly; they should read the classics instead of comics, and so on. Television, the tabloids and pop music have been traditionally regarded by teachers as having detrimental *effects* on the children they teach. This anxiety persists. The media, on the other hand, especially newspapers, have seen it as their prerogative to act as custodians of the nation's moral standards. As apparently self-appointed task-masters, they admonish schools for not doing their jobs properly. When there's violence on the streets, when employers claim that standards are falling, schools are singled out for blame. The media often examine education and their examinations take various forms – from reports by education correspondents in the quality broadsheets to the tabloid exposés of classroom breakdowns and sexual scandals. Then there are the television dramas or drama documentaries. *Grange Hill* is either 'too hard hitting' or 'too soft', depending perhaps on what side of the chalk face you're on. There are also documentaries, such as Angela Pope's 'The Best Days' transmitted in 1977 on *Panorama*, which in turn spread waves of shock-horror through the press.

The media also engage in a form of self-congratulatory reflection. Newspapers print letters addressed to the editor. Programmes like *Question Time* boast the opportunity they give to the public to express on television their views (usually about events which television has constructed for them in the first place). The content of a great many television programmes, especially comedy, rely upon and refer to other television programmes and other media characters. Education does not have even these limited opportunities to reflect upon its own activities. Neither has it the means to do so with comparable visibility. The media are publicly called upon to examine education and even present it as entertainment but the education system is rarely permitted to examine the media. When it does so, the examination is done in terms of media influences and effects on children. These are invariably presumed (though never proved) to be bad and to be guarded against.

Changing the Relations
Teachers have always been *concerned* about the media. The publication of *Popular TV & Schoolchildren* continues that tradition of concern but in reformulations that promise change. The change is not only in teachers' attitudes to the media, but also in the power of schooling to engage with the media on a par more comparable to the power of the media to consider education.

The most substantial reformulation in *Popular TV & Schoolchildren* is the recognition of the sense in which popular television is 'educational':

> It is not possible to separate the responsibilities to educate and to entertain into . . . self-contained boxes . . . education does not stop just because a programme is described as a play, a feature film or light entertainment (p.114 below).

The terms are still those of 'influence' and 'effects' but they have shifted slightly to imply that these effects are not necessarily bad nor are they inescapable. Indeed, the DES Report quotes children's responses to popular TV programmes showing them to be much more alert and critical than the empty ciphers other more 'academic' effects researchers have taken them to be. What the Report argues for, however, is couched in terms of the traditional moral watchdog. Teachers, parents and programme-makers should collaborate, cognisant of their responsibilities as educators all, to ensure that the influences of popular television are beneficial.

71

This relationship between schooling and the media has not been invoked so explicitly before:

There is an undoubted need for arrangements at appropriate levels to enable programme makers, teachers and parents to explore together their different but related responsibilities in understanding better the impact of television upon the young and seeking to ensure that it is a positive and constructive influence' (p.115 below).

The Report calls for more education about television and, by extension, the media more generally. It does not describe, however, what the purposes of such an education should be, nor how it could be effected. I want to attempt some answers to these questions, but it is important to ground them in the context of recent changes in and around the education system which directly affect the state of the curriculum.

Recent History
In 1977, Prime Minister James Callaghan orchestrated a media event at Ruskin College which became known as the 'Great Debate'. Since then, education has become steadily more accountable to the State and resources as steadily cut back. Choices over what and how knowledge should be part of the curriculum have received greater scrutiny, often in terms contrary to the real aims of those in a position to make choices.

Today the autonomy of individual teachers in their classrooms is challenged not from the LEA offices but from Whitehall. As provider and employer, the State now takes more of a controlling interest in education. The aims of social reproduction have to be more explicitly set out by schools and in writing. Since 1977 there has been an unprecedented output of official publications from the DES and from HMI on the school curriculum. There are courses on curriculum studies, directors of curriculum in schools and multifarious curriculum industries springing up.

All this activity has produced even fewer chances for Media Studies in the new curricula. The 1944 Act 'provided secondary schooling for all' but did not set terms for the curriculum. Rather, it provided certain kinds of education for certain kinds of people. The tripartite structure of secondary schools ensured that the upper classes and upwardly mobile middle classes were educated. The working classes in their technical colleges and secondary moderns were trained. I don't want to belittle the achievements of comprehensive education because, given the obstacles, it is clear that a great deal has been achieved. But the basic divisions remain. Some are educated, measured according to their brain power; most are trained, measured according to their man [*sic*] power. And even in mixed-ability classrooms in comprehensive schools there exists an

72

uneasy compromise between academic education and prevocational training.

The academic part of a comprehensive education organises knowledge into discrete subjects. In the same institution it is possible for a different set of students to be channelled into the 'second-best' package courses where more is taught about work discipline than the work itself (understandable, given that most manual jobs now require skills that can be picked up in about three weeks). The school curriculum is designed to teach students the way things are. A teacher's job is, firstly, to inform and, secondly, to instil the 'right kind of values' into students as they receive this information. The processes whereby this instilling and informing are done, the ways in which education is itself mediated, are rarely in themselves questioned, except of course when a teacher introduces explicitly left-wing or right-wing material into the classroom. That teachers claim a neutrality is in itself a political stance, though one evaded and disguised, rarely acknowledged or exposed. This implied side of schooling – the 'hidden curriculum' – is beginning to be more rigorously scrutinised.

I've partly defined the curriculum as what is taught and how. I've mentioned that students are taught about the real world and how to act and behave within it. But teachers, like the media, are unable simply to present the real world to their students. They represent it through the language they use to talk about it, the pictures and examples they use to illustrate it, the exercises they devise to ensure that their representations are received 'correctly'. The education system, like the media, signifies meaning in its own specific ways, bound by a host of pressures and determinations. Any teaching will be influenced by when and how the teacher learned her subject, how she was taught to teach, how her school wishes her to teach, how the inspectors and ministers wish her to teach. There are many determinations outside the classroom. Similarly, a television programme will, however imperceptibly, bear the marks and signs of the production team, the finance department, the forms of individual and institutional censorship. In other words, the knowledge we receive, either through schools or through the media, is constructed in various ways. The ways in which knowledges are compartmentalised, arranged and constructed constitute a curriculum. The present configuration is designed to teach about the way things are, but it is not necessarily 'the way things are' at all. Once it is recognised that schools and the media represent the world to us, that their practices are deeply rooted in particular social and political values, economic exigencies and aesthetics, we are no longer necessarily bound by 'the way things are'.

Arguments for Media Studies
This is where Media Studies comes in. Media Studies can usefully shift

73

the frameworks which bind thinking about what should be taught, to whom and how. Media Studies can aim to make explicit what has hitherto remained hidden in the curriculum; how we come to arrive at the knowledge we have, *given the representations we are given*. Media Studies, through subtle campaigning, should begin to realign what is still a division between education and training.

Peter Gordon has characterised the ways in which knowledge is stratified;

High status as seen in the academic curriculum is characterised as emphasising the literary, a concern with the written rather than the spoken word, abstractness of knowledge structured independently of the learners and knowledge at odds with daily life and common experience.[1]

Low status (i.e. non-academic) curricula are organised, it follows, in terms of oral presentation, group activity and assessment, and concreteness of knowledge. Media Studies can revalue oral presentation, group activity and assessment of concrete knowledge. It can also reassert the importance of the critical by bringing concepts such as 'institution', 'representation', 'denotation', 'connotation' (what Gordon calls 'abstractness of knowledge') to bear on daily life and common experience. Emphasis on the critical is crucial. Too often Media Studies is accorded the low status of a sink option where the 'unteachables' press switches and watch a lot of telly, leaving the others in enough peace and quiet to get on with the 'proper work'.

How to Teach about the Media

The fact is ... if you want to use television for teaching something, you have to first teach somebody how to use television. In this sense, television is not so different from a book. You can use books to teach, but first you must teach people about books, at least about alphabet and words, and then about levels of credibility, suspension of disbelief, the difference between a novel and a book on history, and so on and so forth.[2]

Umberto Eco here points to the need to teach about a visual and auditory literacy, about the construction of suspense, institutional parameters, the different functions of film and television genres, the reasons for different audience evaluations of media products, and many other areas of study.

I have not the space to take up all the possibilities here. A few pointers will suffice. One of the first exercises a Media Studies teacher uses is to show how a single image is an amalgamation of many different 'signifiers' jostling to make their meanings dominant, until the struggle

74

(and our curiosity/perplexity) is put to rest by the caption which 'anchors' (to use Barthes' term)[3] a particular meaning. Additionally, the exercise establishes what particular images or parts of an image signify through a process of elimination. This process, in turn, opens up possibilities of alternatives; not just how things are but how else they might be.

One can then go on to show that, where the media are concerned, no single image is ever permitted to signify on its own. It is always contextualised by captions, where it appears and where it circulates. This raises questions as to what images circulate most, and when and how they are recirculated.

What informs these image exercises is the constructed nature of images and, by extension, all media products. There are no necessarily inherent meanings but rather ones which are perceived as being significant at any given time. The news, for instance, is constructed like any other television programme but none the less most avidly claims the 'truth' as its guarantor. News is made up of stories. So are soap operas. Although the two forms cannot be simply equated, that they both narrate demonstrates how television (like the tabloid press) constantly shifts definitions of what is fiction and what is not. Similar concerns could be demonstrated about media institutions and how they establish constraints and parameters, about histories of popular culture and critical practices, in a movement from image to history, from the particular and the concrete to the general and the abstract.

The Landscape of Media Studies
There is a history to Media Studies. A good place to start would be with the anxiety teachers felt about the 'mass media', an anxiety qualitatively different from the hesitant concern expressed in *Popular TV & Schoolchildren*. The teachers I refer to were university teachers, the notable F. R. Leavis and his student Denys Thompson, who cast themselves in the role of guardians of literary sensibilities and moral values. For Leavisites, the 'mass media' were an encroaching threat. It was seen to be destructive of the elite values inherent in Literature of a certain kind. Since only a refined sensibility could perceive and then scrutinise such values, these were not only elite values, but also elitist. Whereas Literature was 'organic' and the work of an individual, preferably a 'genius', a film or television programme was 'inorganic' in that it had been produced industrially by a team of people. The mass media were technological and industrial, not artistic. The mass media were consumed and relished by the 'mass', not contemplated privately by the solitary reader who, in the act of reading or studying, had to deliberately remove himself from social relations or connections. The mass media were seen as the opiate entertainment, whereas in Literature one could find instruction. These attitudes still prevail.

75

Mike Poole[4] writes about the ways in which such attitudes still dog most of the television criticism to be read in newspapers. They were certainly dominant throughout most of the forties and fifties when the first generations of schoolchildren were provided with some form of secondary schooling under the 1944 Education Act.

But the 1944 Act, by making secondary education for all a legal imperative, meant that the lower social classes had to be educated too. A defensive rearguard action was no longer tenable in the face of this double threat – mass entertainment and education for the masses. Some Leavisite teachers granted that there were some films which could be appreciated, which were works of art rather than industrial products, because they were seen to embody rather than corrupt moral values. These films (mostly European 'Art' films rather than Hollywood 'pap') provided the basis for Film Appreciation courses which became, in turn, a corrective to the new leveller of television. By learning how to discriminate, children would be inoculated against more mechanical influences.

While university teachers found it easy to abstract culture from relations of production, secondary school teachers began to find it rather more difficult. They were, after all, involved in the business of preparing the young for adulthood and the kinds of work and leisure adulthood afforded. In this respect film and television came to be seen as part of Education's responsibility. The Newsom Report[5] in 1963 dealt with 'half our future', the not so academically gifted. Film and television were seen to be useful educational tools but also ones which needed teaching about:

We would wish to add a strong claim for the study of film and television in their own right, as powerful forces in our culture and significant sources of language and ideas. Although the study of these media has for some time been accepted in a small number of schools as an important part of the curriculum, in the majority of schools they are used only as visual aids for the presentation of material connected with other subjects (para 474).

The Newsom Report also saw that film-making – practical activity – was 'interesting and useful' for those who were not educational achievers. But underlying these acknowledgements remained the concern for children as vulnerable beings, as easy prey for the mass media manipulators:

The culture provided by all the mass media, but particularly film and television, represents the most significant environmental factor that teachers have to take into account. The important changes that take place at the secondary stage are much influenced by the world offered by the leisure industry which skilfully markets products designed for young people's tastes (para 475).

A year after Newsom, a book by Stuart Hall and Paddy Whannel was published called *The Popular Arts*.[6] It was intended as a manual for teachers and examined the ways in which popular art – that produced by the 'mass media' – was constituted in relation to the dominant culture. In the early to mid-sixties, then, popular culture (that is to say, culture enjoyed by a large majority), was being rethought, revalued. And in the curriculum the 'non-achievers' had to be provided for. Indeed, the terms of educational 'achievement' were being redefined by a variety of educationalists, from liberal and progressive teachers to the deschoolers. The most pertinent question seemed to be: What is relevant to the child? One of the most obvious answers was – film and television.

Films and television programmes were not considered 'relevant' simply because children watched a great many of them but because they also provided a way into topics which were thought to be more relevant to children's education. They offered windows on to worlds which had hitherto been excluded from the classroom. The progressive emphasis on discussion, on 'theme' work in Humanities, Social Studies, English and Art, allowed teachers to show film extracts which would provoke discussion. The aim was to allow children to find the means and purposes of expressing themselves. It was rarely to change or inform opinion. This kind of approach, epitomised by the Schools' Council Humanities Curriculum Project (1971), was part of more general moves to modernise the curriculum, to imbue it with energy and to save it from the deadening rigours imposed by the grammar schools.

Modernising the curriculum meant making the curriculum more relevant. To make relevant was to modernise. 'Relevance', however, is a very slippery notion. In the later sixties and for most of the seventies, relevance was not seen to extend very much beyond the child itself. In studying film or television extracts, any articulation of a child's response was accepted in the spirit of validating the child as a human being worth taking notice of and worth listening to. Learning how to use ciné cameras or video rovers not only taught technical competence but enabled children to express their own interests through a modern medium. The treatment of children as people worthy of respect is *still* long overdue. Here, however, respect became equated with 'relevance' and it was implied that if only the right kind of knowledge could be taught then things would work out fine for the working-class child. These good intensions beg crucial questions about what is relevant for whom and for what. Where the study or use of film and television was concerned, the provision of what was considered 'relevant' had several consequences that did little more than bring the curriculum 'up to date'.

Use of TV or film extracts rarely included questioning the specific ways in which the medium represented the world. The teaching and learning of technical skills treated both media as transparent. Neither practice allowed for reflection on the specificity of these media.

77

The economic constraints of 1980s recession are far from the optimism of the sixties and early seventies. What is considered educationally 'relevant' has now been redefined and this time it is not teachers initiating redefinitions but central government. Schools and colleges have had to become accountable in economic as well as social terms. Education, unlike business, cannot calculate an end product on the basis of a monetary investment. Nevertheless, educational outcomes are having to be objectified – thus the Assessment of Performance Unit. League tables of exam results have become as important to Heads of comprehensives as to Heads of the competitive grammar and public schools. Ironically, not only does education have to be made accountable for the (less and less) money spent on it but the very terms of that accountability are now defined by business rather than education interests. Courses devised by BEC (The Business Education Council) and TEC (The Technician Education Council) cut firmer edges around vocational/technical courses as well as academic courses set by universities. The BEC/TEC initiatives, however, did allow college departments to tailor units to the specific needs of their own students. Since 1983, it has been the MSC (The Manpower Services Commission), financed not by the DES but by the Department of Employment, which has colonised most of the curriculum space in sixth forms and further education colleges through the YTS (Youth Training Scheme). The space formerly occupied by General Studies and Communications Studies is gradually giving way to Social and Life Skills or Creative and Vocational Planning, where students are offered skills that encourage them to accept their deskilling. These are the spaces into which Media Studies has historically made various inroads but which are now being rapidly blocked. The MSC allows for very little initiative or control at a local level. Pre-vocational education and TVEI (Technical and Vocational Education Initiative) are based on the acquisition of marketable skills. Few courses require or examine capacities to think critically or to produce imaginatively.

The establishment of a core curriculum in secondary schools seems increasingly likely. Since the abolition of the Schools' Council, teachers themselves have had less say in what should be taught and how. The DES paper *The School Curriculum*[7] proposed in 1981 that the broad core should consist of English, Science, Mathematics and Modern Languages. These main subjects would be flanked by Microelectronics, CDT (Craft, Design and Technology) and 'preparation for adult life'. At a time of economic contraction, it seems clear that only those specified subjects will be protected. A subject like Media Studies, which could be part of 'preparation for adult life', will be difficult to argue for. Modernising the curriculum means streamlining it, making it 'relevant' not to the educational needs of students, the failed attempt of the 1950s/60s, but relevant to what a particular kind of economy requires of education.

If Media Studies is going to be useful in educational terms – if it is going to enable students to make informed choices, to develop a critical awareness and to validate their own pleasures – it needs to be understood that holding to notions of relevance or simply modernising the curriculum is no longer enough. I have argued that Media Studies offers new possibilities for challenging the dominant forms of knowledge in the curriculum. Debates about 'relevance' must also focus on questions of how our society is ordered and stratified (how the world is), how we might like those ordered relations to change (how the world could be) and what we need to know in order to make such changes (what would be useful knowledge).

In spite of the fact that debates over educational rationales for Media Studies have been going on for about thirty years now, for many it is still a new subject area. There is not much agreement as to what constitutes Media Studies – indeed the shift from Film or Television Studies to Media Studies marks an important recognition that study of our culture should include all the forms which mediate it. Disagreement also recognises the many relations, whether economic, aesthetic or social, between various media forms. What is clear is that the study of the media requires specific forms of analysis. Televisual literacy is not simply a modern equivalent of literary literacy.

In 1961 Paddy Whannel, then Education Officer at the BFI, complained of 'the lack of a serious critical tradition'. Film, as opposed to Literature or Art History, 'had no clearly defined place . . . within academic education'.[8] But as the subject area became more clearly defined, questions began to be raised as to what defined other, hitherto discrete, areas of knowledge. By asking how *this* subject might be taught, the teaching of other subjects was called into question. The theorisation of Media Studies inevitably implied a retheorisation of educational and critical practices in general.

Sam Rohdie wrote, 'If a film is a new kind of object, requiring its own particular theory, a new discipline with specific methods and techniques, would such a discipline not be challenging to existing theory, to established aesthetics?'[7] It is this challenge to existing disciplines, to existing definitions of knowledge, that Media Studies can make possible. And it is this which makes the notion of 'relevance', as I have described it, irrelevant.

The development of Media Studies theory, amongst other intellectual debates and developments, has made it clear that various knowledges are not naturally compartmentalised into discrete subject areas which the 'academic' or the 'non-academic' child suitably opts for. It has shown how the definitions of what constitutes these knowledges or subject areas are themselves rooted in relations of power. The child who is certificated in the Classics, Humanities, the Sciences, Modern Languages and the Arts is going to inhabit social relations more powerfully

79

than the child who leaves school with qualifications which have merely measured her technical skills. Students are well aware of these knowledge/power relations. What Media Studies can do, by validating popular culture as worthy of study, is to make such relations of knowledge and power more explicit.

Media Studies as a New Order of Knowledge
The ways in which Media Studies theory has converged with theorisations of pedagogy not only challenge existing orders of knowledge but also the ways in which that knowledge is mediated for students. One thing should be clear by now. Knowledge is never simply 'given'. In teaching about the media, teachers have to be aware of and sometimes make explicit their own teaching mediations. We should enable students not just to know more about how the media construct and represent our world but also about the ways by which they are taught. With that awareness, our students can learn that, for example, women are represented in various ways that *could* be different, that a narrative can be constructed variously, that other points of view could be heard on the news. Then they should also become aware that the subjects they learn at school could be taught differently, that there may be other subjects to learn, that there are connections to be made between the subjects they do learn. These general effects I would consider to be part of a general *Media Education*. Media Studies is the term I would use to describe the separate subject area which has struggled for its own space on a timetable. Whether we want Media Studies, a separate subject, or whether we want Media Education as a broader educational objective might be a fruitful subject for debate. I'd be happy with both.

The *dual* educational potential of Media Studies is challenging and exciting. It throws into critical relief the distinction between the theoretical and the practical, the academic and the technical, because it requires both deliberative thought and technical dexterity. It begins to span the great divide between the mental labour of the individual which is given such high esteem in our society and the manual labour of many which is so poorly rewarded.

Conclusion
The separation of theory from practice, of the academic and the technical, which characterises the education system, can be discerned in Lord Percy's question at the head of this article. But it is also possible to argue that it urges forms of combination that are potentially more liberating and less divisive. For those who wish for combination rather than separation, like those who teach about the media, reformulating the terms of Percy's question would be a good place to start.

80

References

1. Peter Gordon (ed.), *The Study of the Curriculum*, Batsford Studies in Education, 1981, p.40.
2. Umberto Eco, 'Can Television Teach?', *Screen Education* 31, Spring 1979, p.15.
3. Roland Barthes, 'The Rhetoric of the Image', in Stephen Heath (ed.), *Image, Music, Text*, Fontana, 1977.
4. Mike Poole, 'The Cult of the Generalist; British Television Criticism 1936-1983', *Screen* Vol. 25, No. 2, March/April 1984.
5. *Half Our Future*, Report of the Central Advisory Council for Education (The Newsom Report), HMSO, 1963(4).
6. Stuart Hall and Paddy Whannel, *The Popular Arts*, Hutchinson 1964.
7. *The School Curriculum*, DES, HMSO, 1981.
8. Paddy Whannel, 'Film Education and Film Culture', *Screen* Vol. 10, No. 3, May/June 1969.
9. Sam Rohdie, 'Education and Criticism', *Screen* Vol. 12, No. 1, Spring 1971.

10. STARTING IN THE NURSERY: WHY TEACH ABOUT TELEVISION?

ANNE HENNESSEY

Most teachers have a professional interest in television, but this interest rarely extends to a concern with teaching about the media. I want here to suggest lines of thought about television and schooling to encourage understanding of the importance of media education for schools. I then want to discuss some of the problems and possibilities of beginning television studies at nursery/infant level.

Notions of Knowledge
What is it that television and schooling have in common? In simple terms, both television and schooling are important and powerful sources of children's knowledge of the world. The question gets more complicated, however, when we consider what we mean by knowledge. Knowledge is often considered as something fixed or absolute which all adults agree about and pass on unproblematically to children. Knowledge is better understood, however, as a *process*, especially as a process of *production*. What I mean to draw attention to by this phrase is the way that schools and television alike are concerned with processes which produce definitions of people, situations, events and relations; that select for emphasis certain meanings and premises; that categorise the world in particular ways; that provide interpretative frameworks for understanding the world. In sum, television and schooling are sites for the construction of *social* knowledge; they are social institutions that have to be examined within the context of the society in which they operate.

Important questions about the nature of social knowledge follow. What views, values, attitudes and beliefs does this social knowledge incorporate? Whose are they? What purpose do they serve? Do schooling and television construct a whole range of views of the world or can we talk of a more limited, central or dominant set of world views? If we can, do schooling and television serve to maintain and legitimate *particular* world views and, therefore, a particular kind of society? What does the social knowledge constructed through schooling and television tell us about society? What do we need to know about society in order to understand these social meanings?

There are clearly no simple answers to questions like these. They do, however, point out useful directions in thinking about television and schooling. Most importantly, they challenge the tendency to see television and schooling as separate from each other and from their society. A focus on the *social construction* of knowledge enables us to consider education in its broadest sense and to recognise television as an educative force. It acknowledges that television, like schooling, has a hidden curriculum. Finally, it enables us to lose the unhelpful distinction between popular/entertainment television and educational television; by this focus, all television can be seen as educative.

As an *institution of knowledge*, television produces *knowledge effects*. These can be understood in terms of the ways in which television provides interpretative frameworks for understanding the world. It is not only effects that we need to be concerned with but also the determinants of television, why television is as it is. We need to know what economic, social and political forces shape media institutions, how media institutions determine messages and how media institutions relate to other institutions. We also need to know more about audiences for television, how audiences make sense of media messages, and whether *audience* as a category is best understood as made up of a mass of atomised individuals or of various cultural sub-groupings. For instance, the category *schoolchildren* may not be the most appropriate when children are considered as an audience, since its use tends to divorce both schools and children from their wider social contexts. Children are also differentiated by gender, class and race, and bring specific sets of cultural orientations to their viewing. These considerations may enable us to clarify the kinds of effects the media might have on individual audience members. They certainly suggest that the study of effects cannot be separated from the study of the media more generally. In order to further knowledge, we need to engage children in Television Studies, not only so that they can consider questions about effects for themselves, but also so that they can begin to develop the analytical skills required for more critical viewing.

Teaching about Television
How best can teachers begin to educate themselves and their pupils about television? It certainly requires teachers to watch popular television programmes, particularly children's programmes, talking to children about what they watch, listening to what children say about television programmes, and grouping together television programmes for study. All of these approaches are only useful, however, as part of a structured Television Studies course. They do not on their own constitute useful approaches, since they produce either endless uninformed discussions or teaching situations where teachers, agreeing or disagreeing with particular viewpoints, get involved in fostering

discrimination in favour of or against those viewpoints.

I would like to suggest that a more useful approach (and one that furthers our understanding of the nature of the relationship between television and schooling) is one that starts by recognising that both schools and television have a tendency to claim that their view of the world can be 'authentic' or 'true'. Implicit here is the notion that the world is a knowable entity, something 'out there' to be discovered, described and explained. It follows from this notion that broadcasters can broadcast objectively and teachers can teach objectively, that school and television messages can be both produced and received by people without viewpoints, and that communication processes are (or can be) transparent. Both schools and television tend to claim an authoritatively realistic representation of the world when in fact their views are highly mediated. The *impression* of immediacy or transparency is important to note because what appears transparent is less likely to be questioned. This tendency, shared by schools and television, is evident in the ways in which television is used in classrooms as a means of teaching about things other than television. The medium itself is rarely the object of study.

As well as providing children with knowledge and using television as a resource for furthering that knowledge, teachers also have to consider how to teach about the construction of knowledge. This will involve examining the question of mediation in the context of both everyday teaching in the classroom and in teaching about the media. For Television Studies, it requires an approach which aims to confront what is specific about the medium and to examine how television does what it does. The aim would be to lay bare television's mechanisms of construction, to question the naturalness of its representations, and to enable children to take a more critical stance. As Len Masterman has argued, teachers need to educate children to a level where they can ask themselves the following questions: 'What does this programme say through its complex system of signs and symbols? What values are embedded here, and what does it tell us of the society in which it finds a place? Who is producing this programme, for what audience, and with what purpose?'[1]

Early Schooling

If a subject is worth teaching, then that teaching must begin during the earliest years of schooling. I finally want to raise some problems and possibilities for beginning Television Studies at nursery/infant level.

The problem of teacher education is a major one for all teachers. How can teachers educate themselves to a level where they feel competent to teach a subject? The problem has additional dimensions, however, when applied to nursery and infant teachers. In the first place nursery/infant teachers are not only subject specialists since they teach a range of

84

subjects across the curriculum to particular groups of children. In the second place, given the ages of the children being taught, progress in any subject is very gradual. A whole school approach to Television Studies is desirable and all nursery/infant teachers need to be educated to a level where they feel competent in teaching the subject. Nursery/infant education, however, is an invisible area at all levels of investigation into teaching the media.[2] Courses on education and the media tend to be geared towards secondary education. There are few detailed analyses of children's television programmes, educational television programmes, and programmes that are popular with young children. Little research has been done on how children learn to watch television and the kinds of enjoyment they get from it. No-one has developed a coherent approach for the teaching of Television Studies to children between the ages of four and seven and there is a lack of teaching materials designed for use with children of this age.

Scholarship needs to address these absences. There is an urgent need for courses at all levels of teacher education and for specialist advisers and qualified inspectors. In the meantime, nursery and infant teachers must seek to educate themselves about television and use what they know about nursery and infant education to develop their own teaching strategies. For instance, since teachers of young children already teach basic skills of literacy and numeracy across the curriculum, they might also teach audio-visual skills across the curriculum. The teaching of literacy skills and visual literacy skills could complement each other and some of the materials used for the teaching of reading could be used to promote visual literacy skills.

This will clearly involve considering the merits of introducing Television Studies as a new curriculum subject. In 1981, the DES recommended that in the primary school curriculum there should be a movement away from narrow 'skills expansion' into the broader areas of humanities, sciences and aesthetics.[3] This was followed by a DES directive that schools must formulate their aims in writing.[4] Given these encouragements, it is obviously important for teachers to articulate why Television Studies is a key curriculum area.

Nursery/infant teachers need also to consider the age category they teach. Since young children are not just watching television but also learning how to watch television, they may not be reading television in the same ways as adults. What are the implications of this for teaching children who are not yet literate? Do children who are not yet literate 'read' television differently? What does a lack of literacy mean in terms of devising methods for evaluating what children are learning about television? Questions like these are important and suggest the need to do more than raid syllabuses designed for use with older children.

At the same time, however, the nursery/infant level of education offers possibilities not always available at other levels. Talk is encouraged in nursery/infant classrooms and teachers – unrestricted by forty-minute periods – have time to talk to children. Children talk a great deal about the television programmes they watch at home, and nursery and infant teachers are usually skilful listeners. They are therefore well placed for learning more about how young children use television. We need to know whether or how these dialogues between teachers and children might provide a basis for developing a coherent and structured approach to Television Studies at the nursery/infant level.

References

1. Len Masterman, *Teaching about Television*, Macmillan, 1980.
2. It is significant to note here that nursery education was the only sphere of schooling not represented by the teachers panel who produced the DES Report *Popular TV & Schoolchildren*.
3. *The School Curriculum*, DES, 25 March 1981.
4. 'The School Curriculum', *DES Circular 6/81*, DES, 1 October 1981.

11. FUTURE DEVELOPMENTS IN TV & MEDIA STUDIES: AN ECOLOGICAL APPROACH TO MEDIA EDUCATION

LEN MASTERMAN

The present period represents, I think, a significant watershed in the history of Media Education in this country. Whereas, over the past fifty years, the important questions facing those teachers with an interest in the media have been largely *epistemological* (being concerned to establish the media as a viable area for study within schools, and media education as a coherent intellectual discipline in its own right with its own characteristic concepts, practices, and modes of enquiry), over the next twenty years or so much more attention will need to be paid to *strategic* questions (that is to questions of legitimation, circulation and dissemination, as well as co-operation, co-ordination and interaction). This is not to assert that media educators now have all of the answers, and no longer need to develop their subject, but it is to suggest that any radical developments within the field are more likely to emerge from an increasing awareness by media educators that media education is most fruitfully thought of as a *lifelong* process, within which other agencies, institutions and individuals will have important roles. I want to suggest in this short paper some of the ways in which a more 'holistic' or 'ecological' approach to media education – an approach which emphasises the importance of *partnership* between those agencies with a legitimate interest in the field – might begin. This will be considered under two general headings: (1) the integration of media literacy/media education as an important element in the teaching of *all* school subjects; and (2) the integration within media education of those agencies with an interest in the field.

1. *Media Education Across the Curriculum*
Apart from establishing Media Education as an important specialist discipline in its own right, media teachers will also need to encourage media education in the teaching of all subjects for a number of reasons:

a) Media materials will increasingly be used in a routine way in the teaching of all subjects, as more of their ostensible content finds its way on to videotape and film. It seems likely that the media will be used, as they have within schools in the past, predominantly as 'transparent' carriers of information, unless media teachers intervene. It is obviously of some importance that they should, if only because their own teaching is unlikely to be effective if it is being actively counteracted everywhere else in the school. One aspect of this issue is particularly relevant at the present time. Hit by severe financial cutbacks, many schools are finding it difficult to provide as wide a range of educational materials as they did in the past, and are beginning to rely increasingly upon glossily packaged and presented film, video and other materials produced by multinational corporations, government departments, and other well-established institutions and agencies. It is a matter of some importance that such material should not be consumed innocently, but read critically. In particular, the basic media literacy technique of relating media messages to the political, social and economic interests of those who are producing them needs to be encouraged as a matter of routine by teachers of all subjects.[1]

b) Media Education across the curriculum needs to go beyond problematising media materials, however. For the media are constantly working over much of the manifest content of school subjects and academic disciplines. All teachers of all subjects might profitably reflect upon the extent to which the effectiveness of their teaching may be materially affected by the images, ideas and stereotypes which already exist in the minds of their students, and of which the media are one of the most powerful sources. So, in the teaching of any topic, the teacher might begin by considering the representations of it with which students are already familiar. Indeed in Geography, the concept of the 'image-region'[2] – those popular ideas, images and representations of, say, China, Europe, the USA or Russia, which exist in all of our minds – is already well established, and would certainly constitute a fruitful point for liaison between geographers and media teachers.

c) Apart from the *content* of different subject areas, the media frequently make statements about the nature of academic disciplines themselves. So any science teacher who wishes her students to challenge the notion of her subject as a largely undisputed body of ideas, theories and facts will need to counteract the messages about her subject suggested by the use of scientists in advertisements or on news and current affairs programmes, to say nothing of the often didactic and expository tone of many 'serious' television science programmes.[3] Similarly, the history teacher who wishes her students to consider the ways in which popular movements of ordinary people have been powerful agents within history, or to give children some sense of their own historical roots, will have to work against the dominant messages about the nature of history of a great deal of historical drama on television, with its emphasis upon

88

great individuals (almost exclusively men), its fascination with royal and aristocratic personages, and its concern with the nation state.[4]

The issues raised here in a vestigial form are already firmly on the agenda for many subject specialists. There are growing bodies of literature and examples of institutional practice which point to highly practical ways in which links between media educators and other subject specialists may be forged. The hard lessons of the general failure of 'Language Across the Curriculum' policies need to be learned however. In particular, the enterprise is unlikely to succeed if it is seen by subject departments as a form of territorial encroachment. In my own institution, a small interdisciplinary team has been formed to look at the possibility of developing coherent approaches to the assessment of media evidence across a wide range of subjects. In the long term there is a possibility that we may be able to develop an attractive and coherent approach to developing media literacy skills in the training of teachers of all subjects. But for the moment, it is enough that the channels of communication have been opened, that dialogue can begin, and that subject specialists have the opportunity of assessing for themselves the relevance to their own subjects of critical media reading skills.

2. A Holistic Approach to Media Education

In arguing for a more integrated approach to Media Education, I will briefly consider four areas (amongst many) in which co-operation seems both possible and advisable: (a) interaction between media educators and parents; (b) interaction between media educators and media personnel; (c) interaction in the training function: in the training of media personnel, and the training of teachers; (d) the development of Media Centres: institutions with a specific remit to encourage interaction and integration.

a) Interaction between Educators and Parents We need to begin by stressing that *some* interaction between teachers and parents is an inevitable part of any Media Education programme. This is because Media Education is a form of curriculum development which will not only be new to most parents, but one which will be especially open to misinterpretation and misunderstanding. For example, the introduction of popular television programmes into the classroom may be regarded by some parents with suspicion and even hostility. Moreover, Media Education constitutes an area in which the school curriculum is likely to impinge upon domestic habits of media consumption.

The media teacher who can generate parental understanding and support, who can take parents into her confidence about her curriculum objectives, and who can work co-operatively with parents and parental groups will find that she has important allies in her task of developing a critical understanding of the media amongst her pupils. A number of approaches to working with parents may be briefly suggested:

Media workshops Such workshops could hope to: (i) raise consciousness amongst parents of the work undertaken in the classroom by the media teacher; (ii) encourage parents to analyse the media and discuss media issues at their own level of sophistication; (iii) suggest concrete ways in which parents could interact with their children.

Viewing Logs Encouraging parents and children to keep a formal record – say for a week – of the child's television viewing (hours of watching, tapes of programmes, programme preferences, etc.) or newspaper reading, can facilitate discussion, encourage the analysis of problems and lead to a positive action programme for both teachers and parents.

Information Resources Teachers can help provide parental groups with information they may need to investigate a problem in an enlightened way. This may involve the provision of accessible digests of research in areas of interest, making available sources of hard information about the media, or providing details of media organisations (and individuals within them) who are receptive to public feedback.

Working within the community The most effective co-operation is likely to develop not by asking parents to come into education institutions after work but by taking workshops, exhibitions and displays into local community bases, such as libraries and community centres.

Reaching Wider Parental and Public Groups Media educators should be particularly adept at using local and national media to their own advantage. Many media teachers will have developed their own contacts within the media, and these can be used to advantage in the coverage of positive developments within media education which can reach a wider audience of parents.

b) Interaction between Media Educators and Media Personnel Very simple steps can be taken to develop fruitful collaboration between teachers and media workers. Many journalists and broadcasters are themselves sharply critical of the dominant practices of their industries and can illuminate them with a specificity which is beyond the scope of most educators. Inviting practitioners into the classrooms is, then, one simple way of initiating collaboration which is well within the reach of all teachers. The local chapel of the National Union of Journalists can be a useful source of contacts for teachers wishing to develop this kind of collaboration. Journalists have also been prominent in the Campaign for Press and Broadcasting Freedom, another useful source of local contacts for teachers.[6]

In working with broadcasters and journalists, however, the teacher will need to ensure that they are broadly sympathetic with her own

90

objectives. For an outing to a newspaper office or a visit from a broadcaster *can* turn out to be a counterproductive exercise, an exercise in public relations which simply reinforces media mystification by drawing attention to the wonders of professional expertise and competence. Close liaison between the teacher and the media professional can help to ensure that this does not occur, but, whenever it does, the role of the teacher is of vital importance in placing the work of professionals within more critical perspectives.

c) Interaction in the training of teachers and media personnel I have already argued that a critical understanding of media processes should be an important part of the training of all teachers whatever their subjects. Broadcasters, journalists, and other media workers can play an important part in this training. Similarly, trainee media workers need to grasp the wider significance of the representations they produce, and to understand the complex ways in which they may be read and used by audiences. Whilst there are some institutions in which the professional training of photographers, journalists and broadcasters is seen as a *critical* as well as a practical activity, in many it is not. There is a strong case for urging that the training of media personnel include media *education* as well as media production if only because, as professionals, they may ultimately be employed in institutions which are indifferent to such concerns.

d) Media Centres This paper has provided a handful of examples of the kinds of productive interchanges possible between agencies and individuals with a stake in the development of media education. Little or no mention has been made of the constructive roles which could be played by media researchers, broadcasting companies, politicians and the public at large. Clearly there is a case to be made for the development of quite new kinds of institutions – Media Centres – which would have a specific remit to encourage the kinds of co-operation outlined here. Such centres might ideally:

(i) be based within the community rather than within an existing 'education' institution
(ii) act as regional focal points for the discussion of media issues, the development of lifelong media education programmes and the integration of those agencies with an involvement in or concern about the media
(iii) develop a resources base, for professionals and public, which would include video-tapes and equipment, films and film equipment, media books, teaching materials, periodicals, research papers, etc.
(iv) organise seminars and lecture programmes for a wide range of participants; these should be principally, though not exclusively, public events and some might be linked to accredited school, college and

University courses
(v) provide training and facilities for the production of community-based newspapers, video and radio, and provide help with the problems of producing, distributing and circulating information for community-based groups and individuals
(vi) draw into media education much-needed additional funding from central government, local authorities, research foundations, arts associations and television and newspaper companies.

References

1. P. Wiegand, see *A Biased View*, University of London Institute of Education, 1982; D. Wright, 'Distorting the Picture', *Times Educational Supplement*, 6 November 1981, p.20.
2. See J. W. Watson, 'The Role of Illusion in North American Geography', *Canadian Geographer*, v.13 n.1; J. W. Watson and T. O'Riordan (eds), *The American Environment: Perception & Policies*, John Wiley, London, 1976; M. J. Youngs, *The AnteBellum South as an Image Region*, Discussion Paper in Geography No. 12, Oxford Polytechnic, Oxford 1980.
3. C. Gardner and R. Young, 'Science on TV: A Critique', in T. Bennett *et al* (eds), *Popular Television and Film*, BFI and Open University Press, 1981.
4. C. McArthur, *Television and History*, Television Monograph 8, BFI, 1978.
5. Any teachers who are interested in developing (or who have developed) similar approaches in their own institutions are invited to contact Len Masterman at the School of Education, Nottingham University, Nottingham, with a view to forming a national network of contacts and experiences.
6. The Campaign can be contacted at 9 Poland Street, London W1V 3DG.

Acknowledgments

Many of the ideas touched on in this paper were discussed in greater depth at an international seminar in which I participated during a UNESCO Conference on the *Media and Society* held in Marseilles in March 1984.

I acknowledge the contributions of all participants in the seminar, and in particular Dr Dorothy Singer of Yale University, and Dr Jean Desautels of the Centre for the Study of Communication and Culture, London.

PART V
THE DES REPORT

POPULAR TV & SCHOOLCHILDREN: THE REPORT OF A GROUP OF TEACHERS

1. Introduction
This study carried out by fifteen teachers was concerned with the images of adult life and society made available to young people in a range of popular BBC and ITV television programmes. It is hoped that its findings will encourage and inform serious discussion of the issues raised among professionals in education and television, parents and the general public.

The teachers were not a representative sample in the strict social scientific sense, though the group was composed with particular factors in mind: there were members from each region in England (but not Wales or Scotland), some from inner city, suburban, town or rural schools; there was a balance of men and women; there was a range of experience from heads through to recent recruits to the teaching profession; there were representatives of each phase of schooling (except nursery) and teachers from the mainstream, special and independent sectors with a variety of subject backgrounds; West Indian and Asian ethnic minority groups were represented. Some had experience of discussing television programmes with their pupils, but none was chosen as an 'expert' or because of a lifetime teaching television appreciation. (A list of the teachers involved is given in Appendix 1.)

The concern of teachers and others involved in educational provision about mass media, and television in particular, is of long standing. It is based on both awareness of their potential as educational tools and anxiety least they be negative influences on the attitudes and behaviour of young people. A considerable amount of research has been done throughout the world on the relationship between television and young people, but few clear-cut, broad conclusions have emerged from such work. Recent studies have suggested that young people between five and fourteen years of age spend an average of twenty-three hours per week watching television, and with this amount of exposure it is difficult to believe that a medium in which so much advertising capital is invested has no influence on young people's attitudes and values. A brief bibliography of relevant material is included in Appendix 2. The present study is short and on a small scale, and it is important to note that the focus of attention is on the content of the television programmes chosen for viewing, and in particular on values, explicit or implicit, within the programmes. Different people may perceive the same television programme in quite different ways and then put that experience to quite different uses. What pupils saw in and gathered from the programmes was therefore of major interest to us. Pupils' views quoted in the text are taken from work done at the schools in which members of the committee teach. But our main primary objectives were to clarify and discuss teachers' views of the programmes. We drew from personal experience as well as professional experience in the classroom for our discussion of the possible effects on young people which the programmes might have.

The Directors General of the BBC and IBA gave their full co-operation and nominated a co-ordinator within the organisation to act as 'link-man' with the Committee, and to facilitate contacts with BBC and ITV producers. The Audience Research departments of the BBC and IBA were also contacted, and provided viewing figures for the programmes and dates requested.

A five-week viewing period between 1 March and 4 April was chosen. The selection of programmes to be viewed from among those available took into account the need to cover the range of types of programme, and the relative popularity of programmes with young people. As our general aim was to gauge the picture of the adult world presented to young people by television in programmes made primarily for adult or family audiences, the programmes selected were from those normally shown at times when such people were likely to be watching, i.e. from about 5.45 p.m. till about 10.30 p.m. For a variety of reasons, but primarily restrictions of time, we decided to omit advertisements, feature films and single plays from the list, although we recognised that each was a rich source of relevant material. After discussion, all members of the group were equipped with a list of questions to be asked of the selected programmes. We also agreed to make a note of particularly striking points which were outside the framework of the questions. Viewing Report Sheets were completed after each programme. (See Appendix 3 for questions and report sheets.)

Finally, producers of some of the BBC and ITV programmes were interviewed. The Editor of BBC 1's *Nationwide* also attended our third meeting and answered teachers' questions on a variety of issues arising from their viewing of the programme. Representatives of the BBC, IBA and ITV companies attended part of our fifth meeting in June and discussed general points of concern raised by teachers.

2. The Programmes
The programmes selected for viewing were:

Drama	*Light Entertainment*
Crossroads (ITV)	Emery (BBC 1)
Dallas (BBC 1)	Family Fortunes (ITV)
The Dukes of Hazzard (BBC 1)	The Gaffer (ITV)
Hill Street Blues (ITV)	The Glamour Girls (ITV)
McClain's Law (BBC 1)	The Kenny Everett TV Show (BBC 1)
Minder (ITV)	Mind Your Language (ITV)
We'll Meet Again (ITV)	Shelley (ITV)
	Top of the Pops (BBC 1)
	Whoops Apocalypse (ITV)

News and Current Affairs	*Science/Features*
Early Evening News (BBC 1)	Tomorrow's World (BBC 1)
ITN at 5.45 (ITV)	Police (BBC 1)
Nationwide (BBC 1)	
Panorama (BBC 1)	
World in Action (ITV)	

Brief details of these programmes are given in Appendix 4.

The percentage of the total UK population, broken into age groups, watching the selected programmes is given in Tables 1 and 2 overleaf. These figures are compiled by Broadcasters' Audience Research Board (BARB), owned by the BBC and the Independent Television Companies Association. Data are derived from a panel of homes in which each television set has a meter attached and each individual household member, aged 4 or over, keeps a diary record (or has one kept) of all his or her viewing in the home. The meter monitors and records the times at which the television set is switched on or off or between channels and the channel to which the set is tuned. This method makes no assessment of the amount of attention given to a television programme by members of its audience, and the figures should therefore be treated with caution. Among interesting features of the tables are:

a) The highest percentage viewing figures appear among the 8-11 and 55-65+ age groups. Adolescents and those in their early 20s presumably have other' things to do such as homework and extending their social lives outside the home. There is also some evidence of differences between adults and children in their programme preferences. Understandable as these are, given the subject matter of the programmes, it means that quite often adults and children in the family will not be watching TV as a group.

b) Light entertainment programmes are most popular with young people, with *Top of the Pops* and *The Kenny Everett TV Show*, scheduled one after the other, attracting the largest audiences. (39% and 31% of all 4-15 year-olds, respectively.)

c) More than one in five young people in each of the age bands between four and fifteen watched *Tomorrow's World*. It is not known the extent to which figures are boosted by its scheduling immediately before *Top of the Pops*. It is interesting to note the dip in audience figures in the 16-24 age group for these three very popular programmes on a Thursday evening.

d) Viewing figures for *Minder* on a weekday and *We'll Meet Again* and *Dallas* at a weekend gave some indication of how many young people may be watching television after the 'watershed' at 9 p.m. No viewing figures within age bands are available for *Hill Street Blues*, but it seems likely from the total viewing figures, and from pupils' comments to the Committee about the programme, that a considerable number of young people watch it. About one in five young people between twelve and fifteen watch *Minder*; about one in seven between eight and fifteen watch *Dallas*.

e) About one in five young people, at all age levels, seem regularly to watch an early evening news programme, and about one in ten between eight and fifteen watch *World in Action*.

3. Issues Arising from the Programmes
Television is not 'a window on the world'. In using broadcasting services 'as means of disseminating information, education and entertainment', in the words of the BBC's Royal Charter, those working in television select, manipulate and allot priorities to the various aspects of society which they choose to broadcast according to changing economic and professional criteria. Among those subjects whose treatment in television programmes is most persistently a topic of public concern are violence and sex.

97

TABLE I

Percentage of total population watching selected television programmes during week beginning 8 March 1982.

	Total Population	Age 4–7	Age 8–11	Age 12–15	Age 16–24	Age 25–34	Age 34–44	Age 45–54	Age 55–64	Age 65–
Monday										
Early Evening News (BBC 1)	13	6	11	9	10	11	11	16	16	24
News at 5.45 (ITN)	17	9	9	12	14	10	10	19	26	31
Nationwide	14	10	11	10	9	13	11	16	16	21
Panorama	8	3	5	3	3	6	7	10	15	17
World in Action	12	3	9	10	10	15	11	13	12	18
Police	16	1	3	7	12	24	19	19	19	18
Tuesday										
Early Evening News	16	9	9	10	12	14	14	18	22	29
News at 5.45	10	10	8	10	13					
Nationwide	13	9	7	7	8	11	12	15	16	20
Emery		14	29	24	17					
The Glamour Girls	15	7	9	9	11	12	10	14	21	27
Wednesday										
Early Evening News	15	14	12	10	9	13	12	17	20	25
News at 5.45	18	8	10	13	16	11	11	22	28	34
Nationwide	10	6	8	8	4	10	8	12	14	16
Minder	24	2	12	22	19	33	26	25	26	31
Thursday										
Early Evening News	16	14	13	13	10	13	14	17	17	25
News at 5.45	18	9	13	14	12	13	13	19	27	34
Nationwide	12	11	9	9	9	13	11	13	14	18
Tomorrow's World	19	20	30	25	16	25	19	17	13	16
Top of the Pops	26	35	48	40	26	34	31	20	13	10
Kenny Everett TV Show	24	23	38	36	21	34	29	22	13	11
Shelley	17	3	9	11	15	21	15	19	20	24
Friday										
Early Evening News	14	12	9	8	8	13	13	15	18	24
News at 5.45	17	13	10	12	15	13	10	20	25	30
Nationwide	12	10	4	6	7	11	11	13	17	19
Family Fortunes	26	23	23	14	18	21	19	26	38	45
The Gaffer	21	15	25	18	15	21	21	22	25	27
We'll Meet Again	21	8	15	13	14	24	22	25	27	26
Saturday										
The Dukes of Hazzard	19	28	29	20	13	19	19	21	20	17
Mind your Language	19	17	16	13	14	18	14	18	21	30
Dallas	20	6	18	13	11	20	18	24	23	32

NOTE: Figures for *Crossroads* and *Hill Street Blues* are not available as these programmes were not nationally networked at the same time.

TABLE II
Percentage of total population watching selected television programmes during week beginning 22 March 1982.

	Total Population	Age 4–7	Age 8–11	Age 12–15	Age 16–24	Age 25–34	Age 34–44	Age 45–54	Age 55–64	Age 65–
Sunday										
Whoops Apocalypse	13	1	6	9	15	20	17	15	11	9
Monday										
Early Evening News (BBC 1)	15	12	13	11	12	12	14	15	17	26
News at 5.45 (ITN)	15	6	9	7	11	11	10	19	25	31
Nationwide	16	14	14	10	12	14	16	17	20	23
Panorama	8	2	3	4	5	7	7	8	12	14
World in Action	14	4	14	9	9	18	16	13	16	17
Police	12	1	2	4	9	19	15	14	18	12
Tuesday										
Early Evening News	13	8	12	10	8	11	13	14	15	24
News at 5.45		7	9	11	12					
Nationwide	11	5	8	8	7	10	10	12	15	19
Emery	18	14	32	19	11	24	19	15	16	15
The Glamour Girls	14	5	7	7	10	12	10	16	22	28
Wednesday										
Early Evening News	13	8	9	9	7	9	11	15	18	25
News at 5.45	17	5	10	12	13	14	10	21	24	30
Nationwide										
Minder	24	3	11	19	22	33	24	28	25	28
Thursday										
Early Evening News	13	9	7	7	7	8	12	15	16	28
News at 5.45	16	5	9	10	12	11	9	19	24	33
Nationwide	11	8	6	8	6	8	10	12	16	18
Tomorrow's World	16	20	25	21	13	19	16	14	14	15
Top of the Pops	25	34	44	33	25	32	28	22	15	11
Kenny Everett TV Show	23	26	36	31	21	31	27	20	12	12
Shelley	20	3	12	12	17	22	18	24	24	30
Friday										
Early Evening News	12	8	9	6	8	8	10	15	16	22
News at 5.45	15	6	11	11	10	9	9	16	23	29
Nationwide	12	8	9	6	8	10	10	13	15	19
Family Fortunes	26	21	25	13	19	23	23	28	34	41
The Gaffer	24	18	31	14	15	24	22	24	25	33
We'll Meet Again	22	7	14	10	14	23	22	26	29	33
McClain's Law	14	3	9	9	9	15	18	17	16	15
Saturday										
Mind Your Language	22	22	20	16	17	21	19	24	27	30
Dallas	23	8	18	16	15	27	21	25	29	35

NOTE: Figures for *Crossroads* and *Hill Street Blues* are not available as these programmes were not nationally networked at the same time.

Violence It would be inconceivable to have television without violence. Its news and current affairs programmes must reflect the violent society in which we live, and its drama programmes stand in a tradition many thousands of years old in which violence is a vital element. But young people are faced by a bewildering range of contexts for physical violence on television; close-ups of the real victims of bomb attacks, the fantasy violence of the animated cartoon, the stylised and sanitised violence of the cops'n'robbers genre, real pictures from international war zones, gratuitous gloating on gory scenes in horror films shown on television, violence genuinely presented as causing pain and injury in fictional programmes which seek to explore its roots in individual or group behaviour. As well as being deeply embedded in human conduct, physical violence may be used as a swift, cheap way of attracting large audiences and may be particularly tempting to the producer or controller competing with others for high viewing figures. It is appropriate that both the BBC and IBA have produced guidelines for producers on the portrayal of violence in television programmes, and the presentation of violence in the programmes we viewed conformed to the guidelines, with two exceptions: an account of a vicious gang assault in *Hill Street Blues* which was narrated in retrospect rather than directly portrayed, and a hand-crushing incident in *Minder*.

In both these episodes the extent of explicit violence went beyond the needs of the dramatic context. There is, of course, physical violence in programmes like *McClain's Law* and *The Dukes of Hazzard*, but it is normally presented within accepted conventions and without gratuitous concentration by the programme's makers. The style of *The Dukes of Hazzard* is slapstick, and though much damage is inflicted on material objects such as buildings, fences and, particularly, cars during and at the end of long chases, the programme may be seen as a modern example of the tradition embodied in the Keystone Cops. For some young people, however, the attractive presentation of reckless driving and car bashing without anyone being harmed in the process may be a dangerous illusion. The excitement felt at the car chases is widespread:

> I like *The Dukes of Hazzard* because I like it when they jump over Roscoe's car. It makes me happy and it makes me excited and I like it when Roscoe's car splits in half because it makes me laugh and I like it when they jump through the window and I like it when Roscoe goes after Bo and Luke (Seven year-old boy).

Hill Street Blues seeks to portray accurately and in detail a seedy, violent society, and the attempts of its local police force to uphold law and order sympathetically. However sensitive its picture of the local environment and of fallible human beings responding to it, however subtle its use of humour to lighten the tone, the programme's approach leads it inevitably to include vivid and frequent images of violence. Even if there is no attempt by the programme to exploit the images of violence, judgements must still be made both about the presentation of single scenes of violence which may be seen by some viewers as models, and about the cumulative impact of the series over a period of time. Young people are aware of the dilemma too:

> I enjoy *Hill Street Blues* because it seems very true to life. In most programmes the good guys never get harmed or injured but in *Hill Street Blues* even the

good guys are hurt and this seems more like real life. Sometimes not everything goes as planned and mistakes happen; this again is true to life, it doesn't always work first time. It can be serious but it has its humour (Fourteen year-old boy).

When violence is shown on the television it is not emphasised enough. If it was shown as if it was real, there would be much more blood. Maybe if they showed a programme where real violence was shown it would decrease the population of violent people, because the violent people would realise what damage they are causing to people (Fifteen year-old girl).

The consequences of physical violence are made clear when it is used in *Minder*, and there is a deliberate attempt to avoid 'sanitised' violence. Although frequently just below the surface, physical violence was not during the viewing period a persistent feature of the programme. When it is included, it does not seem gratuitous and it is normally seen to cause pain and injury. Only when provoked does Terry resort to violence, and then with his fists ('a good clean fight').

My favourite programme is *Minder*. Each programme is packed with fighting, swearing and women. I like Denis Waterman, he is a real hero. The settings are real and the people seem to be just ordinary (Fourteen year-old boy).

It is hard to take seriously, literally, the physical violence in light entertainment, and the accepted context of humour must always be borne in mind. Nevertheless, in two cases the presentation of physical violence was unacceptable: the first is the casual linking of violence with sex in some scenes in *The Kenny Everett TV Show*, and the second the ambivalent and apparently self-indulgent attitude shown to scenes of torture and brutality in *Whoops Apocalypse*.

Scenes of violence and its results were clearly in evidence in news and current events programmes during the viewing period, but overall the preponderance of violence in such programmes reflects on society itself rather than on its reporters. There was some anxiety that the legitimacy of particular causes was being judged by the violence of their supporters' responses, and by the consequent exposure on television of these responses.

Of equal concern is the emotional violence of *Dallas* in which human beings and their feelings are ruthlessly manipulated in the pursuit of wealth and power. The pace of the programme is fast, the production slick: indeed so much happens so fast that any individual human experience is distorted and trivialised because of the superficiality of its treatment.

Pupils themselves have some chilling comments to make on the overall situation:

One of the major forms of corrupting a child is letting him see physical and verbal conflict as an acceptable and everyday occurrence (Seventeen year-old girl).

In violent programmes the fighting and violence never seems to be against the law, and it is always regarded as perfectly acceptable. The television also makes out the men that win the fights and who beat up the other men to be the

101

heroes. In some cases television glorifies the violence and makes it look the right thing to do in a tight situation. This shows young kids that if they get into a difficult patch the thing is to do what *Minder* did last night and beat him up (Fifteen year-old boy).

Violence now is used as another word for entertainment (Fourteen year-old girl).

Watching scenes of violence may in the short term make some young people more aggressive, and it may act as an outlet for others: considerable research has already been done. Long-term effects are less amenable to research, and we are very concerned about the cumulative effect on young people over a period of time of the frequent presentation of violence, in all its aspects. Does it lose its capacity to shock? or develop an appetite for more?

Finally, in feature films shown on television far more explicit scenes of violence and sex are available to young people than were included in the programmes we chose to view. Many pupils report that they stay up late, if necessary, to watch these films and with the present rise in the sales of video recorders the problems of limiting young people's exposure to such material become massive.

Sex In their treatment of sex, television producers face a similar dilemma to the one inherent in the presentation of violence. It is impossible to ignore so powerful and intimate an aspect of human behaviour, yet the temptation to exploit sex is ever-present, either intentionally to shock or titillate, or to attract large audiences, or to win a cheap, knowing laugh. *Dallas* was of considerable concern to us because of its attitude to sex. Sexual intercourse seemed an extension of business practice, the assumption being that sexual intercourse is a normal part of JR's relationship with any woman. A similar idea, that casual sex is now the norm in a relationship between a man and woman, was reinforced in one episode of *Minder*.

Pupils commented that they were embarrassed sometimes when watching television with their families:

Sex is shown in the wrong way. It shouldn't be abused on telly because it is a private thing between two people. We get more embarrassed when it's true sex, but when it's on soap operas, e.g. *Dallas*, you can laugh to cover your embarrassment (Thirteen year-old girl).

A more sensitive description of the developing sexuality of a teenage girl was given in *We'll Meet Again*, but even in this programme there were so many principal characters in the story (well over 20) that there was insufficient time to explore any one relationship in sufficient detail to provide convincing character-isation: the sexual aspects of relationships were not presented in the context of fully described characters.

There were no over-explicit scenes of sex in any of the selected programmes. What was most worrying was the heavy reliance on sexual innuendo in *The Kenny Everett TV Show*, scheduled at a time when many young people must have been watching with their families. The same is true of Bob Monkhouse, compere of *Family Fortunes*.

No serious portrayal of homosexuals was noted in the programmes viewed. The

102

view of homosexuals as camp and effeminate, particularly embodied in the BBC situation comedy *Are You Being Served?*, is confirmed by reference in comedy programmes such as *The Kenny Everett TV Show* where the aim is to raise a quick risqué laugh.

One of the most common ways in which young people approach television is through identification with the characters and personalities whom they regularly watch.

Heroes and Personalities The characters most easily fitting the traditional image of a 'hero' are probably the brave US airmen in *We'll Meet Again*, and particularly their handsome leader, Major Jim Kiley. The programme was produced in a romantic style which tried to create an atmosphere of ordinary people trying to be heroic but being thwarted by a range of human problems.

More popular with young people at the moment are characters who are contemporary versions of the Robin Hood figure: they define their own morality; are unfettered by laws, routine or bureaucracy; dispense justice as they see fit. Something of this character is seen in the heroes of situation comedies such as *Shelley* and *The Gaffer*, but it is at its clearest in drama programmes. The two boys in *The Dukes of Hazzard* cope with injustices as well as the corrupt local 'boss' and his idiot policemen; Jim McClain uses his own methods to bring criminals to justice, even if that means departing from standard police procedures; the methods used by the police in *Hill Street Blues* are unorthodox and tailored to the needs of their local community, as they see them; clearest of all, and most popular with young people to judge from their comments, is Terry in *Minder*. Terry is young, strong, handsome, flawed by a previous spell in gaol but now a warm-hearted protector of the weak or persecuted. His justice is not the remote and impersonal justice of police and law-courts: it is the immediate, spontaneous common morality of fair play for all and particular protection for the weak.

> *Minder* is a very good programme. Every time I see that programme I think that I am going to be like him when I grow up. I'm going to be a minder who minds people who are old or disabled (Ten year-old boy).

While we recognise there is here a positive moral impetus and richness of script, humour and character, there are dangers in presenting so romantic and convincing a picture of the world of petty villainy, and in loading some of the characters in that world with positive values. It is, of course, quite legitimate to suggest that petty criminals may have some positive values and law-abiding citizens some negative ones. But is not *Minder*, in spite of its sharply observed script, its wit, its local London rhyming slang, its excellent casting and production values, a romantic fantasy dressed up expertly as reality? Would Terry McCann remain pure and intact in the real world of petty crime?

All the characters so far mentioned use their powers on behalf of positive values which would be acceptable to many people, who might, however, have some reservations about the apparent lack of loyalty to accepted authority. Another character popular with young people is JR in *Dallas*:

> I like JR because he acts so cool when things go wrong and I like it when he gets

in a temper because his eyes go all small. And I would like to have his money as well, and his power too (Thirteen year-old girl).

JR uses his authority for selfish ends and is happy to manipulate everybody, particularly his most immediate family, in his ruthless pursuit of more money. There are 'good' characters in *Dallas*, such as Bobby Ewing, who embody positive values such as respect for the individual and a sense of proportion in business life. The prevailing impression from the programme, however, is that success is defined in material terms and that in order to achieve that success, deviousness and an utter disregard of other people are legitimate. One of our main concerns about the programme is the potency of the unpleasant image presented by JR, the material success which surrounds his life, and the apparent inability of the other characters in the story to cope with his evil ways.

As far as TV personalities are concerned, by far the most popular is Kenny Everett. It is clear from what young people say that his appeal is based on his versatility and on his irreverence: he is naughty, and says and does rude things.

My favourite is Kenny Everett. His programme is original and he portrays different characters very well, showing his ability (Ten year-old girl).

... I like this programme because he isn't afraid to say anything, he just comes out with it (Fifteen year-old girl).

... the comedy is outrageous ... the sketches he does make me laugh a lot. But to tell the truth some of the sketches he does I don't get the meaning of (Eleven year-old boy).

Such qualities are hardly new (or reprehensible?) in children's entertainment and playground culture, but what is disconcerting is the delivery of cheap smut into the living-room at a time when people of all ages are watching, often in a family group.

Images of Success More intangibly, the general picture of success which emerges is that which is linked with material wealth and power. In different ways programmes as diverse as *Crossroads, Dallas, Family Fortunes* and *Emery* reflected such an emphasis. Although Arthur Daley in *Minder* always gets his come-uppance and his plans are always frustrated, it is clear how he defines his goals of success.

Television also spreads the success of those who are involved in other professions – particularly, perhaps, those in pop music, sport, other forms of entertainment, and politics. Because of its availability, television is a powerful medium for bringing successful people to the attention of the young; but because certain sorts of people are 'good television', the range of qualities seen as desirable is limited. Overall, the view of success presented in the programmes selected was restricted, predictable and lacking particularly the element of altruism.

Attitudes to Authority In approaching the question of how television deals with challenges to authority, the Committee was divided: one man's direct challenge to authority tended to be another's healthy scepticism. The range of programmes in which authority is challenged is wide. On an individual level, both *Shelley* and *The Gaffer* survive by challenging and outwitting bureaucratic authority. Kenny Everett's list of targets include those in real authority and those who assume it (or are assumed to have it): the Queen, politicians, show-biz personalities, the Church, BBC Governors, judges, generals and the police. Authority is corrupt in *The Dukes of Hazzard*, remote and almost irrelevant in *Minder*. The most comprehensive attack comes in *Whoops Apocalypse* where world politicians are caricatured as mad, totally irresponsible, and prepared to do anything to achieve their ends. *Hill Street Blues* explores the nature of authority, gives examples of problems faced by those whose job it is to interpret or enforce the law, as well as portraying the social contexts in which authority is most likely to be challenged.

In the news and documentary programmes, the difficulties inherent in the interpretation and enforcement of law are closely observed in *Police*. Because the professional background of so many people working in *World in Action*, *Panorama* and *Nationwide* is journalism, there is a strong tradition in all of these programmes of persistent investigation, of challenging orthodoxies, of giving support to individuals in their resistance to bureaucracy or big business: the regular *Nationwide* feature 'Watchdog!' is one obvious example, the *World in Action* programme on US Government responsibility for deaths from radiation in Utah another. On the other hand, some challenges to established authority take place in a total context in which traditional values are upheld to maintain the stability of the status quo.

It is clear that television presents a varied and confusing set of messages to young people about authority and the viability of challenge, about ways of distinguishing right from wrong, about ways of relating the images of society to its norms. If the individual is encouraged to define his own values of right and wrong, what happens to the law as a means of support to others? How is the role of the police interpreted?

The Police There are plenty of images of the police in television programmes. In American programmes they range from the gullible, corrupt and inefficient buffoons in *The Dukes of Hazzard* to the earnest, vulnerable and versatile human beings in *Hill Street Blues* who have to work under great stress. Somewhere in the middle comes *McClain's Law* in which the hero's infallibility is not frustrated by normal police procedures and regulations. McClain can escape death at the last minute, or lead the death-defying capture of a criminal, in the best tradition of crime fiction. A typical *Hill Street Blues* episode is noisy, fragmented, with frequent cuts from one sub-plot to another. The main characters are policemen and policewomen, and they are presented as fallible representatives of law and order struggling to uphold their values in a deprived and depressed local community.

> This is not one of your 'dramatic' American cop programmes; it has hard facts and not 'fantasy people' in it like most other American programmes have. It is a real-to-life programme with plenty of action (Twelve year-old boy).

The picture in the contemporary British programmes viewed is different. The philosophy of *Minder* is based on the idea that the normal channels of protection for the individual seem unsatisfactory: police (and other representatives of law and order who appear in the programme) are often corrupt, nasty, ineffectual or irrelevant. During the period after the inner city riots of summer 1981 and the Scarman Report, it was to be expected that examinations and criticisms of police conduct would feature strongly in news and current events programmes. The fallibility of police officers is underlined in the documentary series *Police* and in the public controversy which surrounds it. Amongst the programme's aims were attempts to show the viewing public what the job of policing is really like, and so get people, including policemen, to rethink their assumptions about the way television reflects police work. Such an approach underlines both the fallibility of policemen and policewomen and the range of routine and sometimes unpleasant tasks which they undertake on society's behalf. It is important to remember that even in the cinéma vérité style of *Police* there were limitations on editing: for example, only those police who gave their agreement were shown in the final televised version. Though public opinion polls suggested that adults had found the series valuable and not damaging to their trust in the police, it is not clear how young people perceived the programmes and the subsequent controversy. One pupil wrote:

The police on TV, apart from in the documentary *The Police*, are portrayed as a violent, hard and brutal force, although this comes from plays, for example on riot control. *Nationwide* and other news programmes tend to dwell on their violence. Cell deaths and beatings, false confessions seem constantly in the news. The impressions, therefore, may restrict the police's usefulness as the public may fail to report crimes such as rape. *The Police* documentary on the report of a rape did show their brutal way of treating the woman, disbelieving her to the point where she withdrew the complaint. This aspect of the police definitely needs reporting but excessive reporting destroys the police. Programmes such as *Z Cars, The Gentle Touch, Softly, Softly, Dixon of Dock Green* and *Juliet Bravo* all give a refreshing helpful impression, too admirable in *Z Cars*, for example. There seems to be a lack of realism as they always catch the criminal, always in the right, and so these programmes lose their effectiveness (Fifteen year-old girl).

News and Current Affairs The group considered the methods of presentation in some news and current events programmes (i.e. BBC and ITN Early Evening News, *Nationwide, Panorama* and *World in Action*). How was the separation of fact from comment handled? Was 'balance' achieved? What were the roles of presenters, interviewers and interviewees? Was the time allotted to the subject about right?

There were very few obvious examples of biased or irresponsible reporting during the viewing period. Individual members of the group have differing views on the degree of aggression permitted to interviewers, on the most desirable mix of elements in a programme like *Nationwide*, and on criteria for a subject's inclusion in a news or current events programme. A general trend which caused us anxiety was an apparent policy of presenting an issue as debate between two representatives of opposed position rather than as a more objective analysis or as a discussion involving 'diagonal' thinkers which would keep viewers in touch with complexities not encompassed by the 'for' and 'against' format. What is important is that young people are able to see and understand how television selects and allots priorities to the news it decides to broadcast; what are the contrasting elements of style that differentiate *World in Action* from *Panorama*;

the ways in which a daily magazine programme like *Nationwide* is subject to time and subject pressures which are quite different from those facing a weekly programme like *World in Action*; and the criteria to be used in assessing in as much detail as possible the degree of responsibility a programme is showing in its treatment of a particular item.

Many topics of political significance were covered in news and current events programmes during the viewing period. Four out of five *World in Action* programmes contained political elements: one takes the people's case against the US Government which is accused of causing illness and death from radiation of many citizens in Utah; another, entitled 'Worried Men', examines the views of Tory MPs who have reservations about current economic policies; a third examines the record of the present government of Guatemala, particularly in civil rights; the fourth looks at the resilience of certain pupils in Northern Ireland who, in spite of the political troubles, manage to achieve excellent examination results. During the viewing period, *Panorama* included items on Nicaragua, the political lobby system, the fight for Times Newspapers, extradition laws in Ireland, and Afghanistan, as well as interviews with Robert Mugabe, Mrs Gandhi and David Steel. The national and international ground is well covered. There is also comprehensive coverage, of course, in news bulletins and in *Nationwide*.

At the beginning of this year a new Editor of *Nationwide* was appointed. The programmes during the viewing period were different from the previous *Nationwide* tradition: there were fewer light, human interest stories; more and weightier attention was given to international news; an attempt was made, in two series of films, one about poverty, one about the House of Lords, to explore the broader social context of news rather than constantly being 'summoned by gunfire' to temporary or sensational events. Most of us welcome the move towards more detailed and analytical examination of important news stories; one or two feel that there are already programmes such as *Panorama* which fulfil that role, and that the light idiosyncratic approach of previous *Nationwide* programmes was appropriate to the schedule time and likely family audience. The basic issue remains of how television can give adequate coverage to important subjects, granted its constant need to review priorities in its selection of newsworthy items to be broadcast.

In the first week of the viewing period *Nationwide* included a 'Watchdog!' item claiming the law is an ass because police appear to side with criminals; an analysis of attitudes towards the police in Toxteth, including allegations of repression of blacks by police and employers and suggestions that the riots were externally prompted. In addition in items about rent rebates, a woman allergic to most 20th-century products and about poverty and unemployment, local authorities, the health service, the DHSS and social services were shown to be harsh and uncaring. At the same time there was a constructive and positive feature on the work of the House of Lords.

Politics and Politicians A worrying aspect of this coverage is the unbalanced view of politics and politicians which it makes available. There is a long and honourable tradition of investigative journalism which exists in programmes like *Nationwide* which probe the motives and actions of elected representatives, or stand beside the individual citizen and attempt to assess the effects of political decisions. Nevertheless if the predominant impression offered to young people is

107

that politicians and 'the system' are not to be trusted, that they do not care about society, that they are unsympathetic to the needs of the individual, then there may be risk of disillusionment with democratic institutions and procedures.

Many pupils commented on the fact that they avoided watching programmes on politics:

> If you're interested in politics you can find out quite a bit. Personally I find politics boring so I keep away from them on TV (Fourteen year-old girl).

But the position is not retrieved by the presentation of politics in other sorts of programmes watched, perhaps, by more young people. *Hill Street Blues* presents an example of the frustrating overlap between policing and politics, with politicians presented as publicity-seeking opportunists attempting to thwart the efforts of the humane professionals. *The Gaffer, Shelley* and *The Kenny Everett TV Show* all make scathing references to the motives, speeches or actions of politicians. *Whoops Apocalypse* is an extreme example of cynicism and caricature addressed to the world of politics, where mismanagement, incompetence and greed will inevitably lead to catastrophe.

This is not a case of seeking immunity from attack or caricature for politicians, or indeed for anybody else: but television does present a one-sided picture, with an apparent lack of coverage of those elements in politics which are to do with personal commitment, service to the public, a desire to improve the condition of society through democratic procedures. This is linked with the suggestion of a 'them' and 'us' problem: 'they' represent the government and system and have power, 'we' have no power, cannot effect change and therefore need not become too involved.

In reflecting the society in which it operates, television provides images of various groups which make up that society. We noted the portrayal of several such groups in the selected programmes: families, women, old people, children and young people, the handicapped, ethnic minority groups and foreigners, and the unemployed.

Views of the Family Families are treated in a variety of ways on television. *Dallas* is an example of the family used as a central device to bind together the plot. The intensity of family feeling within the Ewings of *Dallas* is matched only by the intensity of plot and counter-plot between family members. The luxurious lifestyle is not based on common family activity or even in a recognisable home: the Ewings normally get together only at breakfast and for evening drinks, and the locations for these activities might as well be a hotel. The family seems to stay together simply to retain power.

The Dukes of Hazzard portrays traditional aspects of family life, a close-knit group concerned about kith and kin, with relationships strong yet the structure of the family difficult to identify. The family unit supports its members against the outside world.

We'll Meet Again describes the tensions of everyday families under pressure from the cataclysmic events of the Second World War. The social problems shown are easy to identify with – the son who leaves home because he is unable to get on with his father, yet retains his concern for his mother and sister. Family tensions are shown when an affair threatens the stability of the family; problems of disability, attitudes towards pregnancy before marriage – these situations are easily identifiable whatever the period of time.

Crossroads incorporates some contemporary family problems – that of a demoralised unemployed man, for example, or the stresses within an Asian family living and working in the Midlands. Unfortunately teachers and pupils agreed that the poor production of the programme made these portrayals unconvincing and predictable. As far as light entertainment programmes are concerned, aspects of a contemporary family scene are shown in *Shelley* where husband and wife explore modern notions of equality tentatively and with humour. Between Shelley and his wife there seems a natural and unforced warmth of domestic feeling, reflecting a situation not often found in the programmes the Committee viewed: marital contentment. In other programmes such as *Emery*, *The Glamour Girls* and *The Kenny Everett TV Show* occasional aspects of family life are caricatured. *Family Fortunes* celebrated the advertisers' family norm: smartly dressed, happy, white families compete for material rewards, congratulatory of each other in success, sympathetic in defeat. From what pupils say, it seems that the programme involves viewers in the experience of the successful family.

It is difficult to draw conclusions. Certainly there are examples of the positive and fulfilling aspects of family life, as there are of the difficult and sometimes destructive nature of family relationships. Overall, there appear to be few instances, however, in the programmes watched by large numbers of young people where the experience of contemporary families is explored in depth, with sensitivity or with humour. One 17-year-old girl added an interesting view:

> In large families portrayed on TV, e.g. the Ewings in *Dallas*, there are always dramatic conflicts taking place, divorces and affairs and it almost seems as if no family can live in perfect harmony with each other with the exception of *The Waltons* and *Little House on the Prairie*, and both of these exceptions are outdated programmes and therefore this gives us the impression that modern families cannot be united in their family life.

Women There was little in the selected programmes which convincingly reflected the changing role of women in contemporary society: the Asian girl in *Crossroads* and the young wife in *Shelley* were honourable exceptions. In commenting that newsreaders and *Nationwide* interviewers do their job 'beautifully', one member of the group noted that the ambiguity in the word 'beautifully' characterised much of the presentation of women characters in television drama and light entertainment. On the one hand, there are overt protests in some programmes about the sexual exploitation of women, yet on the other some of the programmes' appeal is based on exactly that exploitation. Some of the group felt strongly that the apparent obsession with women's bodies and the reliance on sexual innuendo to get quick laughs in *The Kenny Everett TV Show* reflected overall a degrading and offensive attitude to women.

Just as demeaning to women is the range of roles they are allocated in *Dallas*. With the exception of one, all seem to live their lives through men, who are dominant and manipulative. Women may manipulate men only through their sex appeal: otherwise, they remain flawless ornaments, beautifully attired and always decorative. The growing independence, professional and emotional, of a middle-class woman doctor is one of the main elements in *We'll Meet Again*, and

109

contrasts with other examples in the programmes of more traditional roles for women in the 1940s. Though much of the series seems preoccupied with the American airmen's view of local women as sex objects, there is also a sensitive description of the developing sexuality of a teenage girl as she strives for independence, supported by her mother and brother, and thwarted by her father. Perhaps the clearest portrayal of independent women is in a programme imported from America, *Hill Street Blues*. Two leading characters, a lawyer and policewoman, have strong individual personalities and are presented as the equal of men. Many light entertainment programmes continue to rely on comic stereotypes of women in the seaside postcard tradition. Women do read the News and share in the interviewing and presentation of *Nationwide*. One of the three popular presenters of *Tomorrow's World* is a woman, and the scientific or technological items in the programme do not seem to be allocated to presenters on the basis of any supposed sex bias. Though there are women on the production teams of both *Panorama* and *World in Action*, there are currently no female reporters.

Many young people seem aware of the restricted role allocated to women, particularly in fictional programmes:

Women on TV are always beautiful and well-dressed, such as Sue-Ellen from *Dallas*. If anybody kidnaps or threatens them, someone always comes to the rescue. Women are portrayed as weak and defenceless people (Fourteen year-old girl).

Women are sex objects on telly. Example: men are never seen in the nude but women are (Fourteen year-old boy).

Old People There seems considerable under-representation of old people, with little sense that their age and experience are deserving of attention or respect. They are caricatured as senile in *Emily, Whoops Apocalypse* and *The Kenny Everett TV Show*; an elderly mother-in-law is presented as selfish and cantankerous in *We'll Meet Again*, and in news programmes and *Nationwide* they appear most often as victims or problems. Overall, the opportunity to show the valuable contribution which old people can make to society is being lost.

Children and Adolescents The main image of children and teenagers emerging from news and current events programmes during the viewing period is one of trouble and conflict: the violence of young children in a Toxteth school, for example, or black teenagers' expectations of police violence and corruption. On the other hand a *World in Action* film on young people in Northern Ireland presents them as resilient, hard-working and coping in a very mature way with the civil disturbances there.

Children, like everybody else, are there to be manipulated in *Dallas*. In *Hill Street Blues* their capacity for violence and cruelty is exposed, but often set in the context of adult neglect and urban deprivation. Some of the problems involved in growing up are explored in *We'll Meet Again*, but play no part in *The Dukes of Hazard*.

'Smart' young people take part in *Family Fortunes*; more exotic young people are enthusiastic participants in *Top of the Pops*, which is the most popular of the selected programmes with young people, watched by more than one in three. It presents a cheerful, colourful picture of young people of various ages and races enjoying themselves, with much stress on exotic lighting, clothes and make-up. Its appeal to young people is varied:

I like *Top of the Pops* because one it annoys my dad and two I can get absorbed into it and forget the world problems and my problems (Sixteen year-old boy).

It is a cheerful, musical and colourful programme. They play some good music and you can see the group or singer at the same time which isn't the same as listening to the radio. There are also some good videos that are shown. You can keep track of the latest music and there is a lot of dancing and you can also see the latest fashions that they are wearing. You can sing and dance along with it if you are alone (Sixteen year-old girl).

People with Handicaps The handicapped appeared in the programmes only occasionally, and then as figures either of fun or of menace – or both. The hunchback in *Whoops Apocalypse*, the mysterious limping man in *Emery*, and a one-eared man in *The Kenny Everett TV Show* are three examples. (The second example seems in direct contravention of the BBC's guidelines on 'The Portrayal of Violence in TV Programmes', p.25: 'The use of physical disabilities in association with "bad" characters who may employ violence is almost certainly to be avoided.') We particularly regret the absence of positive images of handicapped people on television because many children are not familiar with handicapped people and may assume the popular stereotype, based in literature and films, which links physical abnormality with behavioural aberration. Occasional coverage in current affairs programmes and an item in *Tomorrow's World* which deals with artificial limbs may provide young people with more information, but may tend to confirm a restricted view of handicapped people as a 'problem'. An attempt is made in *We'll Meet Again* to show the difficulties a man faces in the early stages of disability, having been wounded in the war. His failure to cope with simple things causes tension, and both his need for independence and the responsibilities thrown onto his family, especially the effect upon his wife's conscience, are shown.

Unemployment The unemployed appeared mostly as statistics in news and current events programmes. In human terms television does not yet seem to be reflecting current changes in society, let alone approaching them positively. The emphasis in the situation comedy *Shelley* is not unnaturally on the more light-hearted aspects of outwitting the system rather than on a genuine exploration of the difficulties to be faced.

Ethnic Minorities and Views of Foreigners Representation of ethnic minority groups in the programmes viewed was sparse. *Crossroads* included as regulars a West Indian car mechanic and an Asian businessman, and described some of the problems they face. Blacks appeared in small roles only in *Minder*: a dishonest car dealer, and a gang boss's henchman during the viewing period. They played no part in *Dallas* or *We'll Meet Again*, though it is apparently a matter of history that there were no blacks in the US Air Corps based in Britain during the Second World War. By far the most positive and comprehensive stance was taken in *Hill*

Street Blues, in which a multiracial police force is seen to serve its multiracial community: one of the black policemen, a leading character in the programme, is seen to be both more articulate as a human being and more effective as a policeman than his white colleague.

Young people of all nationalities mix apparently unselfconsciously in *Top of the Pops* but elsewhere in light entertainment programmes the picture is bleak. *Emery* included an episode in which the two detectives are confronted by drunken, black savages engaged in voodoo and eating cockroaches. 'Let's get back to civilisation', said Emery at the end. *Whoops Apocalypse* mocked Islamic law, and *Mind your Language* included a rather ambivalent sequence in which an Asian fails to recognise his own voice because it sounds like a foreigner's. No black families were featured on *Family Fortunes* during the viewing period.

Black newsreaders and interviewers are involved in BBC News, ITN, and *Nationwide*. There are none in the reporting teams on *Panorama, World in Action* or *Tomorrow's World. Police* included a chilling sequence in which an officer described to a class of trainees the supposed racial characteristics of ethnic minority groups. The overall impression gained from news items involving ethnic minority groups was negative, with the focus frequently on conflict rather than any possible contribution they might be making.

Mind Your Language depends for its humour upon the premise that foreigners' language, dress, manners and beliefs are humorous together with their inability to understand English properly. There is no explicit suggestion that the British or their language are superior. Elsewhere stock caricatures abound: Italians in *Emery* are shifty, greasy and unreliable; the recurrent Frenchman, a sort of cross between Charles Boyer and Maurice Chevalier, brings romance to *The Kenny Everett TV Show*; stupid Irish are everywhere; a solemnly efficient German policeman in *Minder* relentlessly pursues his man; and *Whoops Apocalypse* provides a galaxy of different foreign stereotypes. By far the most intensive coverage is of Americans, mainly, of course, through imported American programmes such as *Dallas. We'll Meet Again* attempted a range of American characters, perhaps too many for the time available. Overall, in drama and light entertainment the treatment of foreigners is crude and unsympathetic, all too often sowing the seeds of stereotypes or confirming them.

Again these fictional representations, news and current events programmes provide much factual information, and many contacts with foreign statesmen and their peoples: *World in Action* reported on human conflicts in Guatemala. *Panorama* included an investigation of the real state of affairs in Afghanistan and interviews with Mr Mugabe of Zimbabwe and Mrs Gandhi of India.

All in all, there was a distinct under-representation in the selected programmes of the groups we studied, with too few positive and realistic images of them made available. There was little suggestion of the part they were playing, or might play, in contemporary society, and such treatment as there was in the selected programmes tended to reinforce stereotypes, or link members of these groups to a problem. In giving insufficient coverage to these groups, television is not only giving a distorted view of the society in which it operates; it is also missing opportunities to provide a richer, more varied coverage of human experience and restricting itself to too narrow, well-worn and sometimes trivial a view of life.

Regional Diversity It was unfortunate, too, that the most detailed exploration of regional diversity amongst the programmes viewed was in a programme which does not reflect contemporary life: *We'll Meet Again*, based in East Anglia. There did not seem much attempt to reflect the culture of ethnic minority groups: indeed, *Mind Your Language* may be counterproductive in this. *The Gaffer* in its title and in the flavour of its humour reflects an unspecified area of the North, and *Minder* also attempts through dialect and wit to establish a strong London atmosphere. Weekly general slots and daily *Nationwide* slots are available for viewers to see their own local programmes, but it would be interesting to know the degree to which this arrangement precludes regional items from being shown nationally. Certainly we were disappointed by the apparent lack of diversity in the programmes viewed, and by the strong bias towards the South and particularly London as the source of programme materials.

Views of the Future As for the future, *Tomorrow's World* carried to young people a strong message that science and technology are making the world a better place. Its viewing figures of one in five young people are impressive and as a 'taster' programme covering seven items in twenty-five minutes, it seems excellent. The amount of time allotted allows no more than a brief exploration of the subject so that it is not possible, for example, to describe the social implications of the development. The items are shared between one female and two male presenters, and their approach is cheerful and informal rather than didactic. Attractive and striking visual aids are included, and an atmosphere of suspense and fun is created through the 'live' presentation of the greater part of the programme. What this format makes difficult is conveying a sense of the relative importance of each item, and, often, suggesting to the programme's large audience where it might seek more detailed information. The vast majority of pupils enjoy *Tomorrow's World* and find it interesting.

The other programme viewed which looks to the future was *Whoops Apocalypse*. Its cynical assumption that world leaders are mad and that therefore nuclear war is inevitable certainly painted a depressing picture. Some of us feel that nuclear disaster is not a proper topic for comedy, but those who accept that it may be felt that in spite of some clever ideas and funny one-line jokes, the programme relied too heavily on crude caricature and displayed an ambivalent and rather sick fascination with the violence it portrayed. With no hint of amendment or reform, it lacked satirical bite.

4. Conclusion
a) In the programmes viewed there was a high level of professional and technical excellence and much of the output of BBC and ITV was interesting and entertaining. It is important to bear in mind the quality and acceptability of much of British television, particularly when concentrating on that which is controversial or anxiety-provoking. It is also important, particularly for teachers, to avoid falling into the trap of conferring greater value per se on programmes which set out to educate and inform than on those whose primary aim is to entertain.

b) It became clear in the course of discussions with producers and others working for the BBC and ITV companies that there was little agreement among them about the wider educational influence and possibilities of television. Producers often assumed that any discussion of the educational role of the programmes was an attempt to press them into taking a more didactic stance in their productions. This defensiveness militated against a thorough examination of how programmes of all kinds make available to young people images of the world and in this sense, and often more directly, disseminate information and opinions as well as relaying particular attitudes and values(For a minority of children the products of television may be the main source of significant influence on the way in which their images of certain groups develop: for example, the images of black people built up by those children who never meet blacks in real life.)

c) Despite the work and efforts of the BBC's weekly Programme Review Boards, the regular studies of audience reaction carried out by both BBC and IBA, and of the various advisory groups, there was relatively little evidence among producers of a concerned awareness of just how powerful an influence their programmes may be on the lives of young people. In both the BBC and ITV companies too often it was assumed that if teachers were interested in the educational impact of television then schools programmes must be their main concern. It is not possible to separate the responsibilities to educate and to entertain into such self-contained boxes. Yet it seems that programme makers often do so. As a consequence they fail to recognise or act upon the conflict and continuity between the duties to educate and to entertain. It is this failure to link the two that causes concern to teachers, parents and others. For many outside the professional world of television there is a worrying and obvious contradiction between, for example, the exploration of crime, violence or the causes and consequences of war in programmes intended to educate and inform, and the treatment of these same themes in television drama and light entertainment. There is a desire for balance and some consistency that for most people falls far short of anything that could be described as censorship. But there should be at the least a clearer recognition among those in television at all levels that just as entertainment should not be missing from that which is primarily educational, education does not stop just because a programme is described as a play, a feature film or light entertainment.

d) The arrival of Channel 4, the present video boom and the potential of cable television all underline the urgency with which those working in television must consider their role with reference to children. Already through video clubs young people can have regular access to material which would be unacceptable to many adults; many young people now have access to video recorders which enable them to replay television material however often and at whatever time they choose; American research suggests that the more television channels that are available to young people, the more restricted becomes their taste as they become less likely to try something 'new'. How will broadcasters respond to these future developments, and how high a priority will their educational responsibilities have? In the past producers have too often used the lack of clear and consistent research evidence about the effects of television on young people as an excuse for their avoidance of such questions.

e) Schools, too, must review their responsibilities with reference to young people's experience of television. The fact that most children between five and fourteen spend more time watching television than they do working in a classroom underlines the magnitude of the part which television plays in their

114

lives. There are few aspects of life about which television does not pass on messages to young people. Teachers now know what many of their pupils do in their leisure time, in so far as much of the evening is spent in the common experience of watching the same programmes on television. There are obvious opportunities for teachers to share some of this experience and to put it to constructive use in the classroom. It may be that the nature of the medium makes certain sorts of presentation almost inevitable: the drama series is drawn to 'soap opera', with social context and depth giving way to tortuous personal relationships; the complex industrial dispute is reduced to a personal confrontation between representatives of two extreme positions; previous success and public expectations lead comedy towards stereotypes of character and plot; the normal routine is ignored, the colourful, unusual or controversial is highlighted. It must certainly be part of the educator's responsibility to explain these pressures to young people. In some schools, both primary and secondary, considerable attention has been given to the discussion of television programmes seen at home. Bodies such as the British Film Institute's Education Department and the Society for Education in Film and Television have been offering advice and in-service training to teachers for many years, and a small number of secondary schools have courses in media studies which may lead to public examination at CSE or O level. Both the BBC and ITV have themselves put on television programmes for schools which looked critically at their network programmes, although the present copyright position which among other things makes it illegal for schools to record evening television programmes for subsequent educational use in the classroom is a considerable handicap. But specialist courses in media studies are not enough: all teachers should be involved in examining and discussing television programmes with young people.

f) The vast majority of young people's viewing takes place at home and this lays considerable responsibility on parents to control the amount and nature of the viewing, and to discuss what young people have seen. This is no easy task because young people often have different interests from adults, and in quite properly seeking to cater for those different interests, specific programmes are aimed at particular age groups.

g) Parents and teachers have common concerns about the impact of television on the views and attitudes of young people. The debate about these matters tends to be confined to public confrontation between those taking up extreme positions in respect of particular programmes. There is an undoubted need for arrangements at appropriate levels to enable programme makers, teachers and parents to explore together their different but related responsibilities in understanding better the impact of television upon the young and seeking to ensure that it is a positive and constructive influence.

115

APPENDIX 1
TEACHER MEMBERS OF THE COMMITTEE

Mrs Beverly Anderson, Headteacher, Bernwood First School, Oxford.
Mr David Baggley, CBE, Headmaster, Bolton School, Bolton.
Mr Dennis Bevan, Headmaster, Rose Hill Day Special School, Warndon, Worcester.
Mr George Donaldson, Archbishop Michael Ramsey C of E Secondary School, London SE5.
Mrs Helen Firth, Stanton County Primary School, Stanton, Suffolk.
Mrs Sharon Goddard, Birley High School, Hulme, Manchester.
Mr Michael Harris, The Hayes Primary School, Kenley, Surrey.
Mrs Moni Hyare, Thomas Gray Language Centre, Slough, Berks.
Mrs Adri Kent, Herne Bay Secondary School, Herne Bay, Kent.
Mrs Glenda King, Holy Trinity C of E JM&I School, London SE1.
Mrs Jill Oldham, Portland Secondary School, Worksop, Notts.
Mr David Voller, Tavistock School and Community College, Tavistock, Devon.
Mrs Enid Western, Headmistress, Easton C of E Infants' School, Bristol.
Mrs Betty Williams, Teacher Key Worker, Beaufort County Primary School, Liverpool 8.
Mr Ian Young, Headmaster, Hedworthfield Secondary School, South Tyneside.

APPENDIX 2
SELECT BIBLIOGRAPHY

1. British Film Institute *Television Monographs* (BFI).
2. Cohen, S. and Young, J., *The Manufacture of News* (Constable, 1973).
3. Groombridge, B., *Television and the People* (Penguin, 1972).
4. Hall, S. and Whannel, P., *The Popular Arts* (Hutchinson, 1964).
5. Halloran, J. D., Brown, R. L., and Chaney, D.C., *Television and Delinquency* (Leicester University Press, 1976).
6. Higgins, A. P., *Talking about Television* (BFI, 1966).
7. Himmelweit, H., Oppenheim, A. N., and Vince, P., *Television and the Child* (OUP, 1958).
8. Masterman, L., *Teaching About Television* (Macmillan, 1980).
9. Murdock, G. and Phelps, G., *Mass Media and the Secondary School*, Schools Council Research Studies (Macmillan, 1973).
10. The Open University, *Mass Communication and Society* (Open University Press, 1977).

QUESTIONS TO BE ASKED OF PROGRAMMES VIEWED

These questions are offered as a guide only. Please do not feel bound by them. Important general themes, such as relationships (including sexual relationships), are very relevant.

1. What picture emerges from the programme of:

a)	families and family life	g)	different social classes
b)	women	h)	homosexuals
c)	ethnic minority groups	i)	handicapped people
d)	old people	j)	the police
e)	children and teenagers	k)	foreigners
f)	the unemployed		

Evidence may come from direct representation of people in these groups, or from others' reactions to/comments about them.

2. What clues are given which might contribute to a young person's definition of a hero or of a successful person? Are heroes set in a convincing social context? Are there stereotypes of successful people?

3. What is the range of circumstances in which authority is challenged in the programmes? How are conflicts, physical and/or verbal, resolved? What are the attitudes conveyed (by writer, producer or characters) towards resolution of conflict by physical violence?

4. Does the content of the programme reflect the regional, cultural and religious diversity of Britain? What information is given about these topics?

5. What picture of the future is given to young people in terms of the world of work, the impact of science and technology, the possibility of social change, environmental issues?

6. What information is given about people involved in politics and about the political process generally at local, national and international levels?

7. News and Current Events Supplement
In addition to the questions above, please also consider these with reference to programmes viewed:

a) How was the separation of fact from comment handled?
b) Was 'balance' achieved? If not, in what ways was the programme distorted? If there was debate, was the form of debate appropriate?
c) What were the roles of the BBC/ITV presenters? If an interview took place, what was the interviewer's attitude to the subject(s)?
d) What were the roles of the external experts/spokesmen/interviewees?
e) Was too much/about the right amount/too little time given to the issues? What effect did pressure of time have? Should the total amount of time have been allocated otherwise?

QUESTIONNAIRE

Please classify the strength of your opinion by making a note as follows after each comment on the report sheet:

3. strong view   2. normal opinion   1. tentative judgement

Date	*Programme Title*	*Committee Member*	Whip *(please circle)* 3 2 1

1. Groups (please specify by letter)

2. Qualities of hero/success

3. Attitudes to authority/conflict/violence

4. Regional diversity

5. Picture of future

6. Argument/presentation of issues

7. Politics

8. Summary (*please circle if appropriate*)

Superficial and trivial	1 2 3 4 5	perceptive and in depth
traditional and accepted	1 2 3 4 5	new and challenging
easy to understand	1 2 3 4 5	hard to understand
sympathetic and friendly	1 2 3 4 5	unsympathetic and hostile
wide, mass interest appeal	1 2 3 4 5	narrow, minority interest and appeal
a good programme of its kind	1 2 3 4 5	a poor programme of its kind

9. Any other comments

118

Date	Programme Title	Committee Member	Whip (please circle) 3 2 1

1. Fact/Comment

2. Balance

3. Presenters

4. External guests

5. Time

6. Other comments

APPENDIX 4
THE PROGRAMMES

The programmes selected for viewing by the Committee were:

Drama
a) *Crossroads* (Central). Three times weekly, 6.30 p.m.
Crossroads is a long-established serial based on a motel in the Midlands. It deals with the personal and professional lives of the motel's owners, staff, guests and local community, and is watched regularly by over 25% of the UK population; its audience contains many young people.

b) *Dallas* (BBC 1). Saturday, 9 p.m.
Dallas is a weekly American serial based on the Ewings, a family of oil tycoons.

c) *The Dukes of Hazzard* (BBC 1). Saturday, 5.15 p.m.
Two teenage boys, a girl and their elderly uncle are the heroes of this American comic drama series.

d) *Hill Street Blues* (Most ITV companies). Monday, 9 p.m.
Hill Street Blues is an American series set in a New York police precinct.

f) *Minder* (Thames). Wednesday, 9 p.m.
A crime series, featuring two central characters, Terry and Arthur, and normally set in London.

g) *We'll Meet Again* (LWT). Friday, 9 p.m.
We'll Meet Again is a serial based on the arrival of US airmen in an East Anglian community during the Second World War.

Light entertainment
a) *Emery* (BBC 1). Tuesday, 8 p.m.
This series of *Emery* is different from Dick Emery's previous shows in that it takes the form of a comedy serial, with Emery and friend as detectives hired to find six missing persons.

b) *Family Fortunes* (Central). Friday, 7 p.m.
A quiz which is one of the most popular programmes of all, particularly with younger children and older people. It features a contest between two families, the skill involved being to guess as accurately as possible what other people have answered to questions put to the contestants. Success is rewarded with both cash prizes and a range of consumer goods.

c) *The Gaffer* (Yorkshire). Thursday, 8.30 p.m.
The Gaffer is a comic series built around the talent of Bill Maynard who plays the boss of a small, run-down light engineering firm.

d) *The Glamour Girls* (Granada). Tuesday, 8 p.m.
The Glamour Girls is a situation comedy featuring two young women, of contrasting characters, who work for Glamgirl Ltd. and are required by their boss to promote a variety of products or ideas.

e) *The Kenny Everett Television Show* (BBC 1). Thursday, 8 p.m.
The programme is typically a series of comic sketches, many featuring Everett in a variety of disguises; there is also pop music and dance.

f) *Mind Your Language* (LWT). Saturday, 6.15 p.m.
The basic scene for the comedy series *Mind Your Language* is a language school, and most of the humour derives from the foreign pupils' inability to speak the English language.

g) *Shelley* (Thames). Thursday, 9 p.m.
Shelley is a situation comedy based on the life of a young unemployed man, his wife and their baby.

h) *Top of the Pops* (BBC 1). Thursday, 7.20 p.m.
Top of the Pops is based on currently successful records of pop music. Some of the groups involved mime their records to the studio audience, others have pre-recorded their music on video.

i) *Whoops Apocalypse* (LWT). Sunday, 10 p.m.
Whoops Apocalypse is a situation comedy serial describing the final stages of our world before it is overtaken by nuclear catastrophe.

News and Current Events
a) *Early Evening News* (BBC 1). Weekdays, 5.40 p.m.
ITN at 5.45 p.m. (ITV). Weekdays, 5.45 p.m.

b) *Nationwide* (BBC 1). Weekdays, 6.25 p.m.

c) *Panorama* (BBC). Monday, 8.10 p.m.

d) *World in Action* (Granada). Monday, 8.30 p.m.

Science/Features
a) *Tomorrow's World* (BBC 1). Thursday, 6.55 p.m.
A typical programme includes seven short items, two on film, five live in the studio, about aspects of technological, medical, scientific or environmental progress.

b) *Police* (BBC 1). Monday, 9.55 p.m.
The documentary series *Police* recorded the work of the Thames Valley Police in a style known as 'cinéma vérité'.

INDEX

The index is organised in four categories: persons/characters, publications, institutions and television programmes.